MW00813591

Eat Plants
EVERY DAY

Eat Plants
EVERY DAY

90+ Flavorful Recipes to Bring
More Plants into Your Daily Meals

Blair & Carolyn Warsham

NewSeed
PRESS

Contents

Hi there

Every day, we eat much more than plants. Blair is the chef behind Wildseed, a plant-based restaurant in San Francisco. But he has a thing for sausage biscuits on his days off. His everything-loving palate informed the plant-based recipes for the restaurant and for this book.

While Blair was creating his first animal-free menu for Wildseed in 2019, his newfound enthusiasm for this style of cooking began to work its way into our meals at home. At the same time, we started to notice how much lighter and—dare we say—younger we felt when we avoided eating animal-based products for several days in a row. This is no small claim for two working parents of a toddler.

We also revisited our own outdated notions about plant-based diets, namely that you need to forego certain indulgent pleasures in order to eat this way. We discovered that food like plant-based mapo tofu and mushroom Bolognese could be eyes-rolling-back-in-your-head delicious—even for people like us who fell in love over a seven-course beef dinner at a local Vietnamese restaurant.

The lasting effects of these realizations took root in our lives to different degrees. While Blair still likes to indulge in the occasional steak, I'm stunned to report that I've become a full-blown vegetarian. After fifteen years as a food writer who prided herself on trying literally anything, the positive transformations that have occurred in my life from eating a plant-based diet are too many to list here, and too amazing.

All of this is to say that this book is not solely for the die-hard plant-based (aka vegan) eaters among us. It's for anyone who would like to explore eating more plants.

We are here to share an exciting new approach to plant-based eating that we hope will enrich your life.

We realize the idea of forgoing meat seems impossible for many for many of you. This book does not espouse an all-or-nothing approach. But whether you've been eating a 100 percent plant-based diet for years or you are just dabbling in vegetable-focused meals here and there, we think you'll probably have some fun with this book's perspective on eating plants every day.

HOW TO KNOW IF YOU'LL LIKE THESE RECIPES?

Let me tell you a little more about the way we like to eat. Then you can decide for yourself. If you ransacked our kitchen right now, you'd find all the usual plant-based stuff: piles of organic vegetables and fruits, and proteins like tofu, beans, and spicy Italian sausages from Beyond Sausage. But you'd also find pizza dough, tahini, kimchi, Sriracha sauce, Chinese chile crisp, and miso.

We are inspired by flavors from all over the globe, and the recipes in this book reflect that.

In some cases, they are loose, Californized takes on traditional dishes such as Indian tikka masala or Japanese donburi—all are, of course, designed to fit the plant-based lifestyle. You'll find dal with crunchy chickpeas, curried cauliflower with muhammara, and sweet roasted strawberries laced with star anise. In no way do we pretend to replicate the classic versions of culturally important dishes.

Finally, have you ever ordered a salad only to be greeted with a mound of lettuce, two cherry tomatoes, and a few cucumber slices? Did it make you feel sad? Or even worse, were you ready to rant about your woes on Yelp? Our philosophy of cooking is a direct reaction to this particular brand of disappointment.

Our salads are treasure troves of produce, seeds, and flavor-rich dressings. Our pastas and rice dishes lead with vegetables and protein, not carbs. And even our desserts and breakfasts intersperse healthy doses of fruits and greens. We like to keep it interesting, and we do that by placing vegetables and/or fruits at the center of every dish. If that sounds good to you, you'll probably like a lot of these recipes.

WHY PLANTS MATTER—SOME REAL TALK

We compiled the majority of the recipes in this book while we were sheltered in place in our home in Marin County, California, during the coronavirus outbreak of 2020. As many can attest, it's been a time of incredible discomfort and loss. But the isolation had silver linings for us.

For starters, we are chitchatting with neighbors and talking on Zoom with cross-country friends like we've never done before. Despite our separation, we feel more connection in some ways. Yes, collectively there's more bickering, more drinking, more Netflix. But we are also playing more board games, learning new languages, building furniture, baking bread, and cooking much, much more.

The bonding inherent in preparing a family meal may be the most brilliant silver lining of this whole experience. Even our three-year-old son, James, settles down to focus when the whole family is tearing up kale or mixing a batter. Many of these

HELP! THIS DOESN'T TASTE AMAZING.

You can't remove an ingredient once it has been added to a dish. But you can add to a dish in order to balance out a slightly off flavor profile.

It's bland. Add a pinch of salt, which helps to enhance flavors.

It's too sweet. Blair normally discards half of the batch and makes that half again from scratch with no sweetness. He then combines the two halves and begins adjusting the seasoning from this new starting point. You could also try a squeeze of lemon or a little cocoa powder, depending on the dish.

It's too fatty. Add an acid, like vinegar or lemon juice. If something tastes too fatty in the pan, add a splash of wine and then cook it off.

It's too bitter. Add sweetness. Start with a teaspoon of sugar or balsamic reduction for a savory dish and taste from there.

It's too salty. As with the remedy for too much sweetness, Blair normally discards half of the batch and makes that half again with no salt. He then combines the two halves and begins adjusting the seasoning from this new starting point. You could also try adding a little lemon juice, vinegar, or another acid, depending on the dish.

recipes have grown out of this bonding. They've been sparks of joy amid canceled visits with family and friends, the existential crisis of the restaurant industry, and breakdowns over restrictive daily routines.

Looking further back, I grew up in the 1980s in the Philadelphia suburbs, blissfully ignorant that our food choices weren't exactly the best thing for our bodies or our earth. Capri Sun, Tastykake, and Slim Jim treats regularly flowed through my veins. Almost every Sunday, breakfast included eggs, bacon, and sausage—plus cream doughnuts and sticky buns for dessert. (Yes, we had breakfast dessert. And we loved it.) Blair's childhood in suburban Atlanta wasn't much different. Some of his fondest memories happened at Waffle House.

If you're in our generation, you'll remember how many parents rejected alternative milks and vegetarian sandwiches—with an exaggerated eye roll—as "hippie food." You'll also remember fad diets centering around grapefruit or cabbage soup, and the misleading and fleeting sainthood of "low fat" everything. It's painful to realize that we spent decades collectively consuming with little understanding of what's truly good for our planet and our bodies. But I have to think it was a necessary part of this process.

We have to know, deeply, what doesn't work in order to create what does.

Now, after a few years of living through previously unthinkable natural disasters—deadly mudslides, wildfires that rage the length of a football field per second, floods, droughts, and power outages—many of us feel we can do something to improve our situation here on earth. We hope this book is a small part of the road map.

We've used this time of isolation to envision the food culture of the future—one in which more and more people are motivated to eat from the earth, creating a better life for generations to come. We are enthusiastic about joining the many others who have already awakened to thinking about how food sourcing affects the supply chain and the health of our planet. If you'd like to learn more, we highly recommend two documentaries: Meat the Truth (2007) and What the Health (2017).

We hope this book continues to help people enjoy eating plants every day, even when nobody talks about pandemics anymore. We look forward to a time of peace and togetherness—a time when society has shifted focus to slowing down and finding more purpose and meaning in the precious actions of day-to-day life.

OUR LOVE-HATE RELATIONSHIP WITH RECIPES

Recipes are inherently flawed simply because not all ingredients are created equal. A sauce made with tomatoes from the farmers' market at the height of summer is going to taste different from a sauce made with winter tomatoes from the supermarket. One clove of garlic is not the same size as the clove right next to it. And not all cooks see things the same way; one cook's small onion is the next cook's medium onion. Bananas and potatoes don't come in cookie-cutter sizes—nothing in nature does! Keep this in mind and taste your food often as it is coming together. Because it's highly likely that the tomatoes and potatoes you use are not exactly the same size as the ones we use to test our recipes, you may need to adjust some seasoning here and there. Read the sidebar on page 11 for some guidance. It has suggestions on how to balance a dish if its flavor profile is a bit off.

HOW WE WRITE RECIPES

Blair has been cooking professionally since he was fifteen years old. These recipes apply the working knowledge he's gathered over time. We tried our hardest to simplify cheffy techniques, making them more approachable for everyday cooking. That said, the entire collection spans a range of time investment and skill levels: from ten-minute salads to patience-required pasta dough.

Each recipe includes a note about how we came up with it or why it's included here. And before the methods (except in the Drinks chapter), you'll find a brief section called "The Plan" that summarizes what you're getting yourself into before you begin. Also, if you see something like "ice cream" or "meatball" in a recipe title, please rest assured the recipe is meat-free, dairy-free, and 100 percent plant based. We're placing the focus on all the added flavor these dishes will bring to your life instead of on the ingredients we're leaving out.

HOW WE TEACH

We teach cooking school-approved techniques, but you'll discover some really fun hacks in these pages as well, like a plastic-bag salad spinner. We also offer suggestions for ingredient substitutions when possible, for those moments when you have difficulty finding a certain ingredient or are just too pressed for time to go buy it.

HOW WE COOK

We are attracted to big, bold flavors. That's why Blair is a huge fan of the grill. Char and smoke add great depth and headiness to plant-based meals. Although having access to a grill is not critical, using one does make a difference in how a finished dish tastes. Aside from the emphasis on grilling, the techniques in this book are similar to what you'd use cooking for omnivores.

Our pantry favorites

Blair has tested almost every plant-based product on the American market. Besides gauging these products for taste and quality, there are a few questions he tries to answer before declaring "this is the brand I'm going to stick with": Is the producer going to be around for more than a couple of years? Is the product consistent and readily available?

He's also looking for the product that is as close as possible to the original thing it's replicating in taste, texture, color, and—equally important—the way it behaves in recipes. All of the products meet Blair's criteria. If you can't find them or if you prefer a different brand, use what you find or prefer but be aware the recipes may not turn out exactly as they did for us.

Just Mayo: Blair is a Southerner, so mayonnaise automatically holds a special place in his heart. He grew up putting mayonnaise on grilled cheese, peanut butter-banana, and—of course—tuna salad sandwiches. Any brand other than Hellmann's (known as Best Foods west of the Rockies) was blasphemy. Just Mayo is the cleanest-tasting alternative we can find.

Just Egg: Turns out, mung beans emulsified in liquid have a consistency that's incredibly similar to eggs in both raw and cooked form. In recipes where eggs have a starring role, like omelets or quiches, Just Egg is always our choice. Just Egg takes a little bit longer to cook than hen's eggs.

Bob's Red Mill Egg Replacer: When baking vegan cakes, cookies, doughnuts, or fritters—or making savory dishes like falafel, lentil-rice balls, and more—Bob is the man.

Miyoko's Creamery butter: Thanks to the genius addition of cashew, this non-dairy butter actually browns like real butter, giving it the nutty flavor that other vegan butters cannot produce. All recipes call for unsalted butter.

Tofutti sour cream: Thick, rich, but also—somehow—infused with the mouthfeel of cream, this product is amazing. The fermentation process gives it the tang you want in sour cream.

Spero goat cheese: Made from sunflower seeds and coconut oil, this product is miraculous, with the near-exact taste and consistency of real goat cheese.

Beyond Sausage: We eat these sausages, both the Italian and the bratwurst, almost every week. When you cook them in a frying pan or on the grill, they form a crust reminiscent of regular meat. The texture and flavor are in a class by themselves when compared to other nonmeat sausage products.

Impossible burger: Even though the Impossible burger is sometimes double the price of other vegan burgers, it's worth it. If you'd like to purchase a more budget-friendly plant-based burger, we recommend Beyond or Lightlife brands.

Better Than Bouillon stocks: This brand's no chicken, no beef, and mushroom stock bases are all quick and easy stock options. You'll see these in numerous recipes in this book. We prefer the richer flavor of these products over the vegetable stock.

Joyva tahini: We find many tahini brands to be bitter. This is the only one that not only isn't bitter but also has a slight toasted nuttiness.

Liquid smoke: In the professional chef's kitchen, liquid smoke is typically viewed as a no-no. But at home—when you don't have a smoker or even the twenty pounds of meat to fill the smoker—it's a solid solution. More important than the brand is the way that you administer it. Liquid smoke can quickly overpower a recipe, so use a dropper. We save the ones from liquid vitamins for this use.

Aroy-D coconut milk: In our experience, this coconut milk brand yields the smoothest result in savory recipes and also makes superior coconut whipped cream, which you'll see in several of the dessert recipes in this book.

Kosher salt: Unless otherwise specified, when a recipe calls for salt in this book, we mean kosher salt. Blair usually buys Diamond Crystal. Morton's is fine as well, but it's saltier, so you'll want to calibrate accordingly.

*We are not promoting any of these brands in exchange for freebies or other remuneration. We are recommending them solely because they yielded what we consider to be the best results in our testing. Taste is quite personal, so we encourage you to explore as well!

Soups
& Salads

HEALTH-BOOSTER SALAD WITH SEEDS, BEETS & TURMERIC VINAIGRETTE

Blair developed this recipe for the Wildseed menu in partnership with Alexandra Rothwell Kelly, who is a dietitian with a master's degree in public health. Their goal was simple: pack as many health benefits as possible into one dish and make it taste fantastic. The result includes a gingery dressing with turmeric, black pepper, and olive oil, which together fight inflammation and boost your mood. The mixture of greens and beans is high in fiber and in nutrients that keep chronic disease at bay. Then there are seeds (healthy fats), raw garlic (immunity), beets (lower blood pressure), fennel (lower cholesterol), and too many more essential vitamins, minerals, and nutrients to brag about. The other nice thing about making this salad is that you'll have some leftover dressing and other healthy things, such as hemp hearts (great in smoothies!), lying around the kitchen after you make it.

THE PLAN: Shave the radishes, fennel, and cucumber and leave to soak in cold water as you prep the other ingredients. Blanch the asparagus and green beans. Then make the vinaigrette and assemble the salad.

To begin making the salad, use a mandoline or sharp Y-shaped peeler to shave the radishes, fennel, and cucumber in the amounts specified, then immerse them in a bowl of cold water for 30 minutes. (The cell structure of the vegetables swells as they absorb water, making them sturdy and crunchy for your salad.)

Fill a saucepan about two-thirds full with water and bring to a boil over high heat. Fill a large bowl with ice and water and set it near the stove. Add the asparagus to the boiling water and blanch until bright green, about 2 minutes. Then, using tongs, transfer them to the ice water to stop the cooking. Add the green beans to the boiling water and blanch until bright green, about 3 minutes, then transfer the beans to the ice water and discard the boiling water. When both vegetables are completely cool, drain them and cut crosswise into 1-inch pieces.

To make the vinaigrette, in a blender, combine the vinegar, ginger, turmeric, garlic, salt, and pepper and blend until smooth. Then, with the motor running, slowly add the oil in a thin stream, blending until the vinaigrette emulsifies. You will not need all of the vinaigrette for the salad. Store the leftover vinaigrette in an airtight container in the refrigerator for up to 1 month.

In a small bowl, stir together sunflower, pumpkin, and chia seeds and hemp hearts and set aside to use as a garnish.

Drain the radishes, fennel, and cucumber and pat dry. In a large bowl, combine the asparagus, green beans, kale, spinach, white beans, radishes, fennel, cucumber, beets, bell pepper, onion, and walnuts. Add ¼ cup of the vinaigrette and toss until all the ingredients are evenly coated. Taste and add more vinaigrette if needed.

Divide the salad between two large, shallow serving bowls. Scoop up the ingredients from the bottom of the bowls as needed to have a nice array on top. Garnish with the seed mix and serve.

FOR THE SALAD

2 watermelon radishes, peeled and shaved paper-thin

¼ cup fennel, shaved paper-thin

1 small Japanese cucumber, shaved into paper-thin strips

½ lb asparagus (6–8 spears), woody ends removed

½ lb green beans or haricots verts, ends trimmed

2 tablespoons sunflower seeds

2 tablespoons pumpkin seeds

2 tablespoons chia seeds

2 tablespoons hemp hearts

2 cups packed stemmed and torn Lacinato kale, in 2-inch pieces

1 cup packed baby spinach or chard

1 cup drained cooked white beans or chickpeas

¼ cup cooked and diced red beets

¼ cup thinly sliced orange bell pepper

¼ cup thinly sliced red onion

¼ cup chopped toasted walnuts (see Note, page 33)

FOR THE VINAIGRETTE

¼ cup balsamic vinegar

1 tablespoon peeled and sliced fresh ginger

1 tablespoon peeled and sliced fresh turmeric, or 1½ teaspoons ground turmeric

1 small clove garlic, minced

¼ teaspoon kosher salt

¼ teaspoon freshly ground black pepper

½ cup buttery extra-virgin olive oil

CHILLED SUMMER TOMATO-MELON SOUP

When grassy, juicy peak-season tomatoes pile up on your kitchen counter, do yourself a favor and throw them into the blender with some watermelon to make this chilled soup. Cheesy as it may sound, this is truly summer in a bowl. The ingredients are simple, but the sweet-vegetal-acidic flavor is complex. You might even surprise people with the tomato-melon combo, which is always fun at a dinner party. Feel free to flip the script on this soup by pairing a yellow melon like Crenshaw, canary, or yellow watermelon with yellow tomatoes. Remember, the riper the better.

 THE PLAN: It's so easy! Just blend everything together except the garnishes, then chill, garnish, serve.

In a blender, combine the tomatoes, melon, cucumber, onion, garlic, oil, vinegar, lime juice, kosher salt, and pepper flakes in batches and purée until smooth, about 1½ minutes. Transfer to a covered container and refrigerate until very cold, at least 30 minutes or up to 24 hours.

Taste and adjust the seasoning with sea salt. Ladle into bowls, garnish with the basil, oil, melon, and avocado, and serve.

1 lb ripe tomatoes (San Marzano or heirloom variety), cored and cut into coarse chunks

Cut-up seedless watermelon, in 1-inch chunks

Cut-up peeled cucumber, in 1-inch chunks

2 tablespoons chopped red onion

1 clove garlic

2 tablespoons extra-virgin olive oil

1 teaspoon red wine vinegar

1 teaspoon fresh lime juice

½ teaspoon kosher salt

¼ teaspoon red pepper flakes

Sea salt

FOR GARNISH

¼ cup loosely packed fresh basil and/or mint leaves

2 tablespoons extra-virgin olive oil

½ cup cut-up seedless watermelon, in small dice

¼ avocado, peeled and cut into small dice

SOUPED-UP MISO

The key to great miso soup is the stock. It should taste like the ocean (in a good way) with the slightest hint of smoke. Here, we use kombu, liquid smoke, and plant-based fish sauce to achieve that heady depth. Then we add vegetables, tofu, and noodles to make a healthy, filling meal. You can also make this delicious plant-based miso soup your own by adding different vegetables or substituting rice for the noodles.

 THE PLAN: Prep the vegetables and other add-ons you'll be mixing into the stock and soup. Then make the stock and then the soup and serve.

To make the stock, in a saucepan, combine the water, stock base, kombu, turmeric, ginger, fish sauce, and liquid smoke and bring to a boil over high heat. Quickly reduce the heat to a low simmer and simmer for 2 minutes. Then cover and simmer for 8 minutes longer. This allows the flavors to infuse while minimizing the evaporation of the liquid. Remove from the heat, strain through a fine-mesh sieve, discard the solids, and return the strained stock to the pan.

To make the soup, bring the stock to a boil over high heat. Add the mushrooms and broccoli and cook for 30 seconds. Then add the chard and asparagus and cook until the asparagus are tender, about 1 minute. Ladle out a little stock into a small heatproof bowl, stir the miso into the stock, dissolving it, and then stir the miso mixture into the soup and remove the soup from the heat.

Divide the tofu, edamame, and noodles evenly between two bowls. Ladle the broth and vegetables over the noodles. Garnish with the green onions and nori and serve.

FOR THE STOCK

5 cups water

2 tablespoons Better Than Bouillon no chicken base

2 sheets kombu seaweed, each about 6 inches square

2 teaspoons roughly chopped unpeeled fresh turmeric

2 teaspoons roughly chopped unpeeled fresh ginger

2 tablespoon No-Fish Sauce, (page 161)

6 drops liquid smoke

FOR THE SOUP

½ cup cut-up shiitake caps, in ½-inch pieces

½ cup small broccoli florets

1 cup chopped stemmed Swiss chard or kale or trimmed bok choy

1 cup cut-up asparagus, in 2-inch pieces

¼ cup white (shiro) miso

1 cup diced tofu, in ½-inch dice

½ cup cooked shelled edamame

1 cup cooked soba noodles (from about 2 oz dried)

½ cup thinly sliced green onions, green parts only

1 sheet nori, shredded (optional)

PHO BROTH WITH VIETNAMESE-STYLE MEATBALLS

Laden with spices and herbs, Vietnamese beef pho has long been one of our favorite comfort foods. There was a time when, if we needed to chase away the Sunday scaries, we ordered bowls from a friendly little San Francisco spot called Y&Y Vietnamese Cuisine. But when our hungover, beef-eating days began to disappear. But when our hungover, beef-eating days began to disappear, the soup did not. Blair got energized to make a plant-based version, which brings us to the recipe you see here. It certainly isn't a doppelgänger of the incredible version from Y&Y, but it has the rich flavor profile and ingredients we crave many nights of the week.

 THE PLAN: Make the broth. While it is simmering, make and cook the meatballs and cook the mushrooms and noodles. Strain the broth, then assemble the pho and serve.

To make the broth, turn on a burner on your stove to medium-high and place the ginger and onion halves, cut side down, directly on the burner until they blacken. Set aside.

In a stock pot, combine the star anise, cardamom, coriander, and cinnamon and toast over medium heat, stirring occasionally, until fragrant, about 1 minute. Add the charred ginger and onion, water, stock base, garlic, tamari, fish sauce, sugar, and dried mushrooms and bring to a simmer. Cover and simmer until reduced by one-fourth, at least 30 minutes.

Strain the broth through a fine-mesh sieve and discard the solids. (You may want to keep the mushrooms for fried rice or another use; discard the stems before using.) Return the broth to the stockpot and keep warm.

While the broth is simmering, make the meatballs. In a bowl, combine the meat, green onions, garlic, lemongrass paste, ginger, fish sauce, sugar, pepper, and salt and mix well. Using a 2-tablespoon (1-oz) scoop (or a spoon with a 2-tablespoon bowl), scoop up the mixture and shape into balls. As the balls are ready, set them aside on a platter.

To make the soup, in a dry frying pan, toast the fresh mushrooms over medium-high heat, turning as needed, until lightly golden, about 3 minutes. Transfer to a bowl.

To cook the meatballs, add the 1 tablespoon olive oil to the same pan and place over medium-high heat. When the oil is hot, add the meatballs and cook, turning as needed, until seared on all sides and cooked through, about 6 minutes total. Set aside off the heat.

Fill a saucepan about three-fourths full with water and bring to a boil over high heat. Add the noodles and cook until just tender, according to package directions. Drain and then toss briefly with cold water to stop the cooking. Add the avocado oil to the noodles and toss to prevent them from sticking to one another.

Continued on page 24...

FOR THE BROTH

1-inch piece unpeeled fresh ginger, halved lengthwise

1 yellow onion, halved through the stem end

2 star anise pods

2 black cardamom pods

1 tablespoon coriander seeds

1 cinnamon stick, burned on both ends with a match

2 quarts water

1 tablespoon Better Than Bouillon no beef base

6 cloves garlic, gently crushed with the back of a knife

1 tablespoon tamari

1 tablespoon No-Fish Sauce (page 161)

1 tablespoon organic sugar

⅔ cup dried shiitake mushrooms

FOR THE MEATBALLS

½ lb plant-based ground meat

¼ cup finely chopped green onions, white and green parts

1 tablespoon minced garlic

2 teaspoons jarred lemongrass paste or finely chopped fresh lemongrass (from about 1 stalk, bulb portion only, tough outer leaves removed)

1 teaspoon peeled and minced fresh ginger

1 teaspoon No-Fish Sauce (page 161)

1 teaspoon organic sugar

Pinch of ground white pepper

Pinch of kosher salt

1 tablespoon olive oil

Reheat the broth to a simmer. Divide the noodles evenly between two large soup bowls. Divide the mushrooms, cabbage, carrot, peas, red onion, meatballs, basil, cilantro, and chile (if using) evenly between the bowls, arranging them on top of the noodles. Ladle or pour the hot broth into the bowls, dividing it evenly, and serve right away, with the lime wedges and hot sauce alongside. Provide each diner with a deep spoon (such as a Chinese soup spoon) and chopsticks.

NOTE: You can skip the meatballs and instead add ½ lb extra-firm tofu, cut into 2-inch cubes, to the bowls along with the vegetables.

FOR THE SOUP

½ lb fresh baby shiitake mushrooms

7 oz dried flat rice noodles (banh pho)

1 teaspoon avocado or olive oil

1 cup finely shredded red cabbage

¼ cup shredded carrot

About 16 sugar snap peas

2 tablespoons thinly shaved red onion or green onion (white part only)

2 fresh Thai basil sprigs

4 fresh cilantro sprigs

1 jalapeño chile, cut crosswise into ⅛-inch-thick slices (optional)

Lime wedges for serving

Hot sauce of choice for serving

SPRING PEA SOUP
WITH SESAME GRANOLA

One of the first things Blair and I shared a love for was shiso! I'm not saying that's when I *knew* he was the one, but it was a big step. You may recognize shiso as the serrated-edged green or purple leaf often adorning sushi plates. It's used as a garnish here too, adding its blend of mint, basil, and just a touch of anise flavor.

Using savory granola to garnish this soup gives it a wow factor and a delicious crunch. (It's always fun to tell guests you're serving granola as part of dinner.) We often add tofu, edamame, or white beans to this soup to make it more of a meal. The granola recipe here makes more than needed. Use the remainder to top salads or Asian-inspired noodle or rice dishes or as a snack.

 THE PLAN: Make the granola first, then the broth and soup. Let the soup chill in the refrigerator while you prepare the garnishes.

To make the granola, preheat the oven to 300°F. Line a sheet pan with parchment paper.

In a bowl, combine all the ingredients, mix well, and then spread the mixture in a even layer on the prepared pan. Bake the oat mixture, stirring once or twice during the baking, until golden brown, 25–30 minutes.

Let cool completely on the pan. The granola will keep in an airtight container at room temperature for up to 2 weeks.

To make the broth, combine all the ingredients in a blender and blend until thoroughly mixed.

To make the soup, add the peas, mint, parsley, lemon zest, and oil to the broth in the blender and blend on high speed until smooth. You may need to leave the blender running for a few minutes to achieve a smooth, uniform consistency. Season with salt, then strain the soup through a fine-mesh sieve into an airtight container. Cover and refrigerate until very cold, at least 2 hours or up to 24 hours.

Taste and adjust the seasoning with salt if needed. Ladle into bowls and garnish each serving with the avocado, olive oil, and lemon juice, dividing them evenly. Top each bowl with 2–3 tablespoons of the granola and a sprinkle of the shiso and serve.

FOR THE GRANOLA

1 cup organic old-fashioned rolled oats

½ cup pumpkin seeds

½ cup sesame seeds

¼ cup poppy seeds

¼ cup pure maple syrup

½ teaspoon kosher salt

2 tablespoons rice bran, grapeseed, or other neutral oil

1 teaspoon toasted sesame oil

FOR THE BROTH

1 teaspoon Better Than Bouillon no chicken base

2 cups water

3 tablespoons soy sauce

1 tablespoon raw cane sugar

FOR THE SOUP

3 cups frozen peas (two 10½-oz bags)

½ cup loosely packed stemmed fresh mint leaves

½ cup loosely packed fresh flat-leaf parsley leaves with stems, roughly chopped

Grated zest of 4 lemons

¾ cup extra-virgin olive oil

Kosher salt

FOR GARNISH

½ avocado, peeled and cut into ½-inch cubes

1½ teaspoons extra-virgin olive oil

1½ teaspoons fresh lemon juice

¼ cup loosely packed stemmed fresh shiso leaves, torn into small pieces

CURRIED SQUASH SOUP
WITH DATES & SEEDS

Squash soup in the wintertime is a classic—if not obvious—move, but we like to make it interesting by punching up the spices and garnishes. With extra curry powder, ginger, and unexpected accents like dates and the seeds of pomegranate and pumpkin, this soup is more of an eye-opener than the typical butternut squash soup.

 THE PLAN: Cut everything, then sauté all the aromatics and seasonings. Add the squash and liquids, simmer, and then purée, strain, garnish, and serve.

Heat a large pot over medium heat. When the pot is hot, add the oil, garlic, ginger, turmeric, salt, and onion and sauté, stirring frequently, for 2 minutes. Add the curry powder and cinnamon and continue to cook, stirring often, for 2 minutes longer to toast the spices.

Add the squash, stock, coconut milk, and lemon juice, stir well, and bring to a gentle boil over medium heat. Reduce the heat to low, cover, and simmer until squash is fork-tender, about 15 minutes.

Remove from the heat and let cool slightly, then, working in batches, transfer the soup to a blender and purée on high speed until creamy and smooth. As the batches are ready, pour through a fine-mesh sieve into a clean saucepan.

Reheat the soup over medium heat, stirring occasionally to prevent scorching, until piping hot. Taste and adjust the seasoning with more curry powder, salt, and lemon juice if needed. Ladle into bowls, garnish with the pumpkin and pomegranate seeds and dates, and serve.

NOTE: If you cannot find fresh turmeric, substitute 1½ teaspoons ground turmeric and add it with the cinnamon.

2 tablespoons coconut or olive oil

4 large cloves garlic, roughly chopped or smashed

2 tablespoons roughly chopped fresh ginger, peeled if desired

1 tablespoon roughly chopped fresh turmeric, peeled if desired (see Note)

1 teaspoon kosher salt

1 large yellow onion, roughly chopped

1½ tablespoons curry powder or Thai yellow curry paste

¼ teaspoon ground cinnamon

6 cups peeled and chopped butternut squash

2 cups Better Than Bouillon no chicken stock

1 can (14 oz) light coconut milk, preferably Thai Kitchen brand

Juice of ½ lemon

FOR GARNISH

¼ cup toasted pumpkin seeds

¼ cup pomegranate seeds

¼ cup Medjool dates, pitted and diced

HEARTY CORN SOUP WITH MISO, BROWN BUTTER & BLACK-EYED PEAS

Here, traditional Japanese seasoning meets Blair's Southern upbringing. The combination of earthy black-eyed peas, sweet corn, and savory miso makes for a beautiful trilogy of flavors. All that said, the secret ingredient here is really the stock. It's what gives depth and richness to so many soups. Finish each bowl with a healthy handful of the crunchy chickpeas on page 165 and you've got yourself a super-satisfying, yet light meal.

THE PLAN: Cut and measure all the ingredients, then cook the corn, onion, and celery together in a pan. Add the liquid and toss everything into a blender to make the soup. Serve, garnish, and impress.

In a saucepan, melt the butter over medium-high heat until it begins to foam and brown. (Miyoko's butter browns when it cooks, so if you use another brand, you may miss the toasty extra layer of flavor you get from browned butter.) Reduce the heat to medium or medium-low (depending on burner strength). Add the corn, onion, celery, and salt and sauté until the onion is translucent, about 10 minutes. Scoop out ½ cup of the vegetables and reserve for garnish, then add the garlic and continue to sauté until all the vegetables are tender, about 5 minutes longer.

Add the water and stock base, then bring to a boil over high heat. Temper the miso by ladling out a little stock into a small heatproof bowl, stir the miso into the stock, dissolving it. Remove the stock from the heat, add the tempered miso, and let cool for a few minutes.

Working in two batches, transfer the soup to a blender and blend until very smooth. Return the soup to the saucepan and heat over medium heat, stirring to prevent scorching, until piping hot. Taste and adjust the seasoning with salt.

To serve the soup the regular way: In a small bowl, whisk together the lemon juice and oil. Ladle the soup into individual bowls and garnish with the beans, reserved corn mixture, green onions, and lemon juice-oil mixture, dividing them evenly.

To serve the soup the fancy cheffy way: In a small bowl, whisk together the lemon juice and oil. Arrange the beans, corn mixture, and green onions in the center or off to one side of each individual bowl, dividing them evenly. Ladle the soup around the garnishes, then dress each serving with an equal amount of the lemon juice-oil mixture.

SWEET CORN TIPS: When you cut the kernels off the cob, they go everywhere. This technique will keep them all in one place: You'll need one roughly cup-size bowl or coffee cup, one large bowl, a kitchen towel, and a sharp knife. Invert the smaller bowl in the middle of the large bowl so the bottom is facing up. Cover the inverted bowl with a folded kitchen towel. This will keep your knife from nicking the bowl as you work. Stand the ear of corn, stem end down, on the towel-topped bowl and cut downward, removing the kernels and rotating the ear a quarter turn after each cut. As you cut, the large bowl collects your bounty.

One of the biggest bonuses to using corn on the cob is corn milk, which lies at the base of the kernels. It's thick and sweet, adding extra depth to a dish. After shucking the ear and cutting the kernels from the cob, run the back of the knife blade along the length of the cob to scrape the remaining bits of corn and the milk-like liquid clinging to the cob directly into a bowl.

2 tablespoons Miyoko's unsalted butter

2 cups fresh or frozen yellow corn kernels (from about 3 large ears)

1 cup diced yellow onion

½ cup diced celery, in roughly ½-inch pieces

½ teaspoon kosher salt

3 cloves garlic

3 cups water

1 tablespoon Better Than Bouillon no chicken base

¼ cup white (shiro) miso

FOR GARNISH

2 tablespoons fresh lemon juice

3 tablespoons grassy extra-virgin olive oil

1 cup drained canned black-eyed peas, rinsed

¼ cup thinly sliced green onion, green part only

HOT TIP FOR IMPATIENT TYPES: Instead of adding the water to the pot while this soup is cooking, fill a quart-size measuring pitcher with ice to the 3-cup line, then add water to get the desired volume. You can pour this into the soup after it boils so you don't have to wait as long for it to cool down. It'll blend all the same!

10-MINUTE ARUGULA SALAD WITH CITRUS, FENNEL & AVOCADO

We adore this combination of tart, juicy citrus and creamy, vegetal avocado. Then in come the perfumy, fancy licorice notes of fennel to make this combination feel a little more adult. You know what else is adult? Getting dinner on the table early enough so you have plenty of chill time later in the evening. This salad should take only about ten minutes to put together.

 THE PLAN: Segment the citrus. Make the vinaigrette. Then cut the fennel and avocado and toss everything together.

To segment the citrus, using a large, sharp knife, cut a thin slice off the top and bottom of the grapefruit. Stand the fruit upright and, following the contour of the fruit and using even, downward strokes, cut off the peel and white pith in wide strips, rotating the fruit after each stroke. Use a paring knife to remove any remaining pith. Now, holding the fruit in your nondominant hand over a bowl, cut along each side of the membrane between the segments, capturing the freed segments and any juice in the bowl. You will need ½ cup grapefruit segments. Then segment 1–2 oranges the same way to yield ½ cup segments. Drain off the juices from the bowl into a small bowl.

To make the vinaigrette, add the salt and lemon juice and zest to the citrus juices and whisk to combine. Then whisk in the oil until emulsified.

Cut off the stalks and feathery green tops, or fronds, from a fennel bulb and set aside the fronds for garnishing the salad. (We save the stalks for soups and stocks.) Halve the bulb lengthwise, then trim away any discolored parts at the base or on the outer layers. Thinly shave the fennel crosswise on a mandoline, or thinly slice with a chef's knife. You will need 1 cup sliced fennel. If needed, trim and slice the second bulb. If you have time, soak the sliced fennel in ice water for 1–2 minutes. The pieces will begin to curl, adding a little volume and texture to the salad. Drain and dry the fennel.

In a bowl, toss together the citrus segments, fennel slices, avocado, and arugula. Drizzle with the vinaigrette and toss to coat evenly. Garnish with the fennel fronds and serve.

1 grapefruit

1–2 oranges (enough to yield 1/2 cup segments)

½ teaspoon kosher salt

2 tablespoons fresh lemon juice

Grated zest of 1 lemon

3 tablespoons extra-virgin olive oil

1–2 fennel bulbs (enough to yield 1 cup thinly sliced)

1 cup cubed avocado, in ½-inch cubes

3 cups loosely packed arugula

MISO KALE CAESAR WITH GRILLED VEGETABLES & CRUNCHY CHICKPEAS

We abandoned traditional Caesar dressing a long time ago in favor of this version with umami-packed miso. This dressing has all the richness of the classic, but it's made entirely from plants. Grill whatever vegetables you like. We use asparagus, peas, and mushrooms in the spring; zucchini, eggplants, and peppers in the summer; and parsnips, fennel, and rutabagas in the fall and winter. Focus on using what is at its seasonal peak and you won't go wrong. Blair prefers to use the grill for this dish because it imparts great flavor, uses less fat, and it makes it easier to cook the vegetables so they remain a bit crisp. But if grilling is not possible, roasting the vegetables in the oven or cooking them in a sauté pan will also get the job done.

THE PLAN: Make the dressing and clean the kale first, then grill the vegetables and assemble the salad. If the chickpeas are not already on hand, preheat the oven when you prepare the grill and roast them while the grilled vegetables are cooling.

To make the dressing, in a blender, combine the tofu, miso, Parmesan, mustard, lemon zest and juice, garlic, and oil and blend until smooth. Season with a healthy sprinkle of salt, then blend one more time to incorporate. Set aside until needed. You will not need all of the dressing for the salad. Store the leftover dressing in an airtight container in the refrigerator for up to 1 month.

To cook the vegetables, prepare the grill for direct cooking over medium-high heat.

Strip the kale leaves from their stems. Discard the stems or save them for another use. (They are quite tasty grilled.) Tear the leaves into bite-size pieces, immerse them in a large bowl of cold water, then lift the kale out of the water and place it on a kitchen towel to drain for use later (Or use a salad spinner to dry the kale.) Or you can use the fun DIY centrifuge method detailed in the sidebar on page 32. (Tip: If your kale is looking a little wilted and sluggish, soak it in a bowl of ice-cold water for at least 20 minutes or up to 1 hour. It will absorb water and spring back to life.)

Trim your chosen vegetables, peel any that need it, then cut into strips that are both large enough to maneuver easily on the grill and won't fall through the bars of the grill rack. For example, if you go with zucchini, split each zucchini lengthwise into quarters. In contrast, once the tough ends are trimmed off of asparagus spears, the spears are grilled whole. (You will cut all of the vegetables into bite-size pieces once they are cooked.) Toss the cut vegetables with just enough oil to prevent them from sticking to the grill rack and season them with salt. (If you use too much oil, it will drip down onto the fire, causing flare-ups that will impart a bitter flavor.)

Arrange the vegetables directly over the fire and grill, turning as needed to cook evenly. Allow them to cook on each side until they are cooked 90 percent of the way through: soft on the outside but still snappy in the center. As the vegetables are ready, pull them off the grill and place them on a plate to rest and cool. They will cook a bit more—the other 10 percent—while resting. Then cut the vegetables into bite-size pieces.

Continued on page 32...

FOR THE DRESSING
¾ cup silken tofu

¼ cup plus 1 tablespoon white (shiro) miso

¼ cup grated plant-based Parmesan cheese, preferably Violife brand (see Note page 32)

1 tablespoon whole-grain mustard

Grated zest of 1 lemon

Juice of 2 lemons (about ¼ cup)

1 clove garlic

½ cup extra-virgin olive oil

Kosher salt

FOR THE VEGETABLES
1 bunch Lacinato kale

½ lb each of three different vegetables at their seasonal peak (see headnote for suggestions)

Olive oil for coating

Kosher salt

¼ cup grated plant-based Parmesan cheese, preferably Violife brand, for garnish

1 cup Crunchy Chickpeas (page 165)

To assemble the salad, put the kale into a large bowl and start to dress it by drizzling 2 tablespoons of the dressing around the circumference of the bowl. Then, using your hand, swirl the kale in a circular motion so it picks up the dressing from the side of the bowl. Dressing the bowl, not the salad, ensures you don't end up with a soggy salad. The amount of dressing you end up using is a question of preference, so add more, a little at a time, if needed.

Divide the dressed kale evenly among individual salad bowls. Garnish each bowl with the grilled vegetables, Parmesan, and chickpeas, dividing them evenly, and serve.

DIY SALAD SPINNER: You may laugh, but this is an awesome hack for making a salad spinner at home using a plastic produce bag and a paper towel. Line the bottom of the bag with the paper towel and place the wet greens on top. Poke a hole about ¼ inch in diameter in the bottom of the bag to create an escape route for the water. Now you're all set to create your very own lettuce centrifuge at home! Hold the bag with your fist at the top to close it and then swing it around and around in a big circle. Feel free to shake your hips at the same time. A little water does come out of the bottom of the bag, so be sure to position yourself in an area where you don't mind a few sprinkles.

NOTE: You can use another brand of plant-based Parmesan. We like Violife because it comes in a block, so you can grate it or shave it just before you add it to the dressing or salad, which ensures a fresher flavor.

SMOKY SALAD WITH HONEY-SHERRY VINAIGRETTE

The marriage of sherry, honey, almonds, and smoked paprika makes for a heady salad. If you're up for buying two different types of almonds, Blair loves using Marcona almonds for the salad and conventional blanched almonds for the vinaigrette. (Skin-on almonds would give the dressing a slightly bitter flavor.) Marcona almonds have a softer texture and a slightly more buttery flavor than the average almond, making them the undisputed queen of almonds among chefs.

We like to use jarred teardrop peppers for this salad because they're a little sweet, a little briny, and bring just a touch of heat—not to mention they look like jewels dotting your lettuce greens. If you cannot find them, jarred roasted red peppers, cut into strips, are the best substitute.

THE PLAN: If you don't have the clover blossom honey or coconut bacon on hand, make that first. (Luckily, that's pretty easy to do.) You need to toast the almonds next. Then, make the vinaigrette, clean the greens and cut the tomatoes, and finally, assemble the salad.

To make the vinaigrette, in a blender, combine the vinegar, honey, garlic, and paprika and blend until smooth. Add the salt and blend briefly to incorporate. Then add the oil and blend until smooth. Finally, add the blanched almonds and blend until smooth. You will not need all of the vinaigrette for the salad. Store the leftover vinaigrette in an airtight container in the refrigerator for up to 1 month.

Butter lettuce is far more delicate than a heartier green, such as kale, so be as gentle as you can when rinsing the leaves. Cut the leaves from the stem and immerse them fully in a large bowl of cold water. Then lift the leaves out of the water and place them on a towel to drain for use later. If you have a salad spinner, it also works great for drying the leaves. Or you can use the fun DIY centrifuge method detailed in the sidebar on the opposite page. (Tip: If your lettuce is looking a little wilted and sluggish, soak the leaves in a bowl of cold water for at least 20 minutes or up to 1 hour. The leaves will absorb the water and spring right back to life.)

Cut the tomatoes into halves or quarters, depending on their size. (If cutting into halves, see the sidebar on page 37.) A good rule to follow is to make sure each piece fits into half of a tablespoon.

To assemble the salad, put the lettuce into the largest bowl you have (to avoid crowding) and start to dress it by drizzling 2 tablespoons of the dressing around the circumference of the bowl. Then, using your hand, swirl the lettuce in a circular motion so it picks up the dressing from the side of the bowl. Dressing the bowl, not the salad, ensures you don't end up with a soggy salad. The amount of dressing you end up using is a question of preference, so add more, a little at a time, if needed.

Divide the dressed lettuce evenly among individual bowls. Top with the tomatoes, bacon, Marcona almonds, and peppers, dividing them evenly, and serve.

FOR THE VINAIGRETTE

¾ cup sherry vinegar

2 tablespoons Clover Blossom Honey (page 153)

2 cloves garlic

1 tablespoon smoked paprika

1½ teaspoons kosher salt

1½ cups extra-virgin olive oil

¼ cup blanched almonds, toasted (see Note)

1 head butter lettuce

½ cup cherry tomatoes

1 cup Coconut Bacon (page 156)

½ cup raw Marcona almonds, toasted (see Note)

¼ cup jarred teardrop peppers or roasted red pepper strips

NOTE: Skin-on regular almonds can be used in place of the Marcona almonds. To toast the nuts for this recipe, or the nuts for other recipes, spread them in a single layer on a sheet pan, place the pan in a cold oven, preheat the oven to 300°F, and toast until the nuts are fragrant and have taken on a little color, about 20 minutes.

10-MINUTE WATERMELON, CUCUMBER & BASIL SALAD

Here's a quick and easy salad to make on repeat all summer long: a cooling mix of sweet watermelon, cucumber, and a little red onion and basil to ground it in reality. (This is not dessert after all.) The dressing features Aleppo pepper, which has an earthy depth that is underpinned by a mild level of spiciness and a little sweetness. Just wait until you taste it with watermelon and cucumber. Gold. This recipe also allows you to indulge in the enjoyable task of smashing a cucumber. Have fun.

 THE PLAN: Cut and soak the onion. Make the vinaigrette. Cut the remaining ingredients. Toss together and serve.

Cut the onion in the amount indicated, then immerse the onion in a bowl of cold water and set aside while you prepare the rest of the ingredients. This cold-water bath will soften some of the astringency of the raw onion.

To make the vinaigrette, in a small bowl, stir together the poppy seeds, salt, honey, Aleppo pepper, lime juice, and oil. It's okay if it's not emulsified.

Using a rolling pin or the flat side of a large chef's knife, press down on the cucumber to flatten it, breaking the skin so it cracks. (Please do not turn it into a pancake.) Dice the cucumber across the grain into ½-inch pieces. Measure 1 cup diced cucumber for the salad. Reserve the remainder for another use. Tear the basil leaves into 1-inch pieces. (Tearing basil instead of cutting it keeps the cell structure from rupturing, preventing the leaves from turning black.)

Drain the onion and pat dry. In a bowl, combine the onion, cucumber, watermelon, and basil. Drizzle with the vinaigrette, toss to coat evenly, and serve.

¼ cup julienned red onion

2 teaspoons poppy seeds

½ teaspoon kosher salt

1 teaspoon Clover Blossom Honey (page 153) or agave nectar

½ teaspoon Aleppo pepper

2 tablespoons fresh lime juice

2 tablespoons extra-virgin olive oil

1 Japanese or English cucumber

¼ cup loosely packed fresh basil or mint leaves

2 cups cut-up seedless watermelon, in 1½-inch cubes or wedges

ARUGULA, AROMATIC CHEESE & FRUIT SALAD

The best salads provide a good balance of nutty, fruity, acidic, bitter, and rich flavors. This one fits the bill. The vinaigrette goes a step beyond the classic lemon juice–olive oil combination and works on almost any salad. To make it, you'll purée dried apricots directly into the vinaigrette, giving it body while softening the acidity.

 THE PLAN: Assuming the onions are already pickled, start by making the croutons, then make the vinaigrette. Cut the pear, crumble the cheese, and assemble the salad.

To make the bread croutons, preheat the oven to 300°F. Put the bread cubes into a bowl, top with the oil and salt, and toss to coat evenly. Spread the cubes evenly on a sheet pan and bake, stirring once halfway through baking, until brown and crispy on the outside, about 20 minutes. Set aside to cool. You will need only 1 cup croutons for the salad. The remainder will keep in an airtight container at room temperature for up to 5 days.

While the croutons are baking, make the vinaigrette. In a blender, combine all the ingredients and blend until smooth and emulsified. You will not need all the vinaigrette for this salad. Store the leftover vinaigrette in an airtight container in the refrigerator for up to 1 week.

To make the salad, combine the pear and arugula in a bowl. Crumble the cheese on top, using your fingers to break it up gently. Add the onions, 1 cup of the croutons, and ¼ cup of the vinaigrette and toss gently. Taste and add a little more vinaigrette if needed.

Divide the salad between two individual bowls, arranging the pear, cheese, and croutons mostly on top, and serve.

FOR THE CROUTONS

1 ½ cups cubed seeded baguette, in ½-inch cubes

3 tablespoons olive oil

Pinch of kosher salt

FOR THE VINAIGRETTE

1 tablespoon chopped dried apricots

½ cup fresh lemon juice

¾ cup extra-virgin olive oil

1 teaspoon kosher salt

½ cup diced Asian pear

2 cups loosely packed arugula

½ cup Miyoko's winter truffle cheese or other semisoft aromatic plant-based cheese

¼ cup Pickled Onions (page 154)

LITTLE GEM SALAD WITH AVOCADO & GREEN GODDESS DRESSING

Green goddess dressing is a San Francisco legend, having been created at the city's Palace Hotel in the 1920s. Blair likes to think of it as a slightly lighter, more herbaceous version of the ranch dressing in which he was basically baptized in the South. We make our version lighter and more healthful than the original by using tofu. From a nutrition standpoint, this salad has it all: protein from tofu and hemp hearts, healthy fats from avocado and olive oil, and fiber from the greens.

 THE PLAN: Make the dressing. Mix the seeds. Prepare the remaining toppings and assemble the salad.

To make the dressing, in a blender, combine the green onions, parsley, tarragon, basil, garlic, salt, pepper, onion powder, oil, lemon juice, and vinegar and blend until smooth. Add the tofu and blend until fully incorporated. Set aside. You will not need all of the dressing for the salad. Store the leftover dressing in an airtight container in the refrigerator for up to 1 week.

To make the seed mix, in a small bowl, stir together all the ingredients. Scoop out ¼ cup of the mix for the salad. The remainder can be used for dressing up salads, soups, and even pasta dishes. Store in an airtight container at room temperature for up to 1 month.

Peel the radish, cut into paper-thin slices, and then immerse the slices in a bowl of cold water until needed.

Put the lettuce into a large bowl and start to dress it by drizzling 2 tablespoons of the dressing around the circumference of the bowl. Then, using your hand, swirl the lettuce in a circular motion so it picks up the dressing from the side of the bowl. Dressing the bowl, not the salad, ensures you don't end up with a soggy salad. The amount of dressing you end up using is a question of preference, so add more, a little at a time, if needed.

Divide the greens evenly among individual salad plates and flatten them out. Divide the seed mix evenly among the plates, sprinkling it on the lettuce. Drain the radish slices and pat dry. Top the lettuce and seed mix with the remaining ingredients—radish, avocado, tomatoes, and cucumber—in layers, dividing them evenly among the plates, then serve.

NEVER CUT CHERRY TOMATOES THE SAME WAY AGAIN: All you need for this fun trick is a large, sharp serrated knife, a cutting board, and two identical circular plastic lids from a couple of to-go containers. Invert one lid on a cutting board and place the cherry tomatoes on the lid. Place the second lid right side up on top. Now, with your nondominant hand, apply gentle pressure to the top lid, pinning the tomatoes between the lids. Using the knife, cut the tomatoes in half as they're held in place by the lids, steadily moving the blade parallel to the board from one side to the other. How amazing is that?

FOR THE DRESSING

½ cup sliced green onions, green part only

½ cup roughly chopped fresh flat-leaf parsley (leaves and stems)

¼ cup loosely packed fresh tarragon (leaves and thin stems)

¼ cup loosely packed fresh basil leaves

1 ½ teaspoons minced garlic

1 ½ teaspoons kosher salt

1 ¼ teaspoons freshly ground black pepper

½ teaspoon onion powder

½ cup extra-virgin olive oil

1 tablespoon fresh lemon juice

1 tablespoon red wine vinegar

½ cup silken tofu

FOR THE SEED MIX

¼ cup flaxmeal

¼ cup chia seeds

¼ cup hemp hearts

2 tablespoons Maldon sea salt

1 watermelon radish

2 heads Little Gem lettuce, leaves separated and left whole

1 ripe avocado, halved, pitted, peeled, and diced

10 cherry tomatoes, halved (see sidebar)

½ Japanese cucumber, halved lengthwise, then cut crosswise into ½-inch-thick half-moons

ROASTED EGGPLANT
& NOODLE SALAD

This dish hits every note in the flavor lexicon and is shockingly balanced. Sweet, sour, salty, spicy, umami, smoky, nutty, herbaceous—all of them are here, plus the intoxicating contrast between velvety eggplant and crunchy peanuts. Boom! You are going to love it.

If you've never tried fire-roasted eggplant before, give the blow-torch technique a try. It's a bit laborious, but it transforms the humble eggplant into a miraculously flavored and textured treat. And did we mention you get to use a blow torch? (This is Blair's favorite eggplant cooking method for many reasons!) Don't worry if you don't have a blow torch. We provide two other methods that also work well.

 THE PLAN: Make the sauce. Cook the eggplant. Then cook the noodles, blanch the green beans, and ready the remaining ingredients just before plating.

To make the sauce, in a blender, combine all the ingredients and blend until smooth. Set aside, unstrained, until needed. The sauce can be transferred to an airtight container and refrigerated for up to 24 hours before straining.

Char the eggplants using one of the following three methods. The first, Blair's favorite, calls for a blow torch and tongs. Using the tongs, hold an eggplant at arm's length with your nondominant hand. Holding the torch in your other hand, turn the torch on and hold each side of the eggplant in the flame, rotating the eggplant as needed, until the eggplant is charred and blackened on all sides, 15-20 seconds on each side. Repeat with the remaining eggplants.

The second method calls for a gas stove and tongs. Turn a gas burner on medium-high. Using the tongs, place an eggplant directly on top of the flame. As soon as the skin on the underside is charred, carefully rotate the eggplant with the tongs to char the next side. Continue to rotate as needed until the skin is charred and blackened on all sides, 15-20 seconds on each side. Repeat with the remaining eggplants.

The third method calls for the broiler, a sheet pan, and tongs. Preheat the broiler. Arrange the eggplants on the sheet pan and place the pan on the top rack in the oven directly under the heating element. Watch the eggplants closely and rotate them as soon as they begin to blister and char on each side. (You do not want to leave the eggplant in the oven any longer than needed because the interior will overcook.)

Once the eggplants are charred and blackened on all sides, transfer them to a large bowl, cover the bowl with a plate or plastic wrap, and let sit and steam for about 10 minutes. This steaming will help further loosen the skin from the flesh.

Using a paring knife, gently remove the skin from the eggplants, wiping off any stubborn black char with a wet paper towel as you go. Now cut the eggplants into 3-inch-long logs and pull the logs apart, like string cheese, into quarters. Set aside.

Cook the noodles according to the package directions, drain, rinse with cold water, and set aside.

FOR THE SAUCE

1 cup No-Fish Sauce (page 161)

⅔ cup water

⅔ cup fresh lime juice

½ cup rice vinegar

⅓ cup raw cane sugar

¼ cup chopped lemongrass (bulb portion only, tough outer leaves removed)

2 cloves garlic

1 tablespoon Sriracha sauce (optional)

2 lb Japanese or Chinese eggplants

¼ lb bean thread noodles

½ lb long beans or green beans, trimmed and cut into 2-inch lengths (about 1 cup)

2 cups loosely packed stemmed fresh mint leaves

2 cups loosely packed small fresh cilantro sprigs

1 cup loosely packed stemmed fresh Thai basil leaves

1 cup cherry tomatoes, halved (see sidebar, page 37)

¼ cup ground peanuts

¼ cup fried shallots or onions, such as French's brand

Fill a saucepan about two-thirds full with water and bring to a boil over high heat. Fill a bowl with ice and water and set it near the stove. Add the beans to the boiling water and blanch the long beans for 1 minute or the green beans for 2 minutes. Drain the beans and transfer to the ice water. When the beans are completely cool, drain them. Cut the beans into 2-inch lengths.

Strain the sauce through a fine-mesh sieve. In a bowl, combine the noodles, mint, cilantro, and basil, add ½ cup sauce, and toss to coat evenly. Add more sauce if needed in order to completely coat all the ingredients.

Transfer the dressed noodles to a serving platter or divide among individual plates. Arrange the tomatoes, beans, eggplants, peanuts, and fried shallots on top and serve.

Mains

GREEN CURRY VEGETABLES
WITH STICKY BLACK RICE

This recipe is a weeknight go-to dinner that allows for endless substitutions. The main components are a spice-laden, Thai-style curry broth, an abundance of cooked vegetables and protein, bright raw garnishes, and sticky rice. This ingredient list displays our favorite vegetables to use, but please substitute whatever you like.

Now about that sticky rice (aka glutinous rice or sweet rice). It gets its name because it's especially sticky when cooked. Preparing it takes a bit of extra effort, as you need to soak the raw rice in water for at least 2 hours to ensure it cooks evenly. The finished product is unparalleled in its ability to soak up sauce, making the extra step worth the time. We use sticky black rice here, which is higher in antioxidants, fiber, vitamins, and minerals than its white counterpart; however, jasmine or brown rice is a fine substitute in this recipe.

THE PLAN: Soak the rice for at least 2 hours, then cook it. Choose the vegetable add-ins you will be using, then clean, cut, and measure them and all the other remaining ingredients. Next, make the curry paste and build the curry broth. Finally, stir in the broth add-ins, cook, garnish, and serve.

To cook the rice, put it into a sieve, submerge the sieve in a large bowl filled with water, and then lift out the sieve and discard the cloudy water in the bowl. Repeat at least four or five times, using fresh water each time, until the soaking water runs relatively clear. Now soak the rice, still in the sieve, in water to cover for at least 4 hours or up to overnight to saturate the grains. (You can shorten the process to only 2 hours by soaking the rice in hot water.)

Remove the rice from the water. The grains should be much softer and a little swollen. Transfer the rice to a bamboo steamer basket or a metal colander. You may need to line the basket or colander with cheesecloth, depending on the size of the perforations. Select a pot that will accommodate the basket or the colander and fill it with water, making sure the water level is at least 2 inches below the bottom of the basket or colander. Place the pot on the stove top and bring to a boil over high heat. If using a steamer basket, place the lid on the basket, and set the basket on the pot. If using a colander, set the colander in the pot above the water (or rest it on the pot rim) and cover the pot with its lid or aluminum foil.

Steam the rice for 15 minutes. Test a few grains to make sure they are soft and fluffy. If they are still a little crunchy, steam for a few more minutes. When the rice is ready, transfer it to an airtight container or hold it in the covered basket or colander off the heat until ready to eat.

Continued on page 44...

1 cup sticky (glutinous) black rice

FOR THE CURRY PASTE

1 tablespoon coriander seeds

1 teaspoon cumin seeds

1 tablespoon peeled and roughly chopped fresh turmeric, or 1 teaspoon ground turmeric

2 lemongrass stalks, bulb portion only, tough outer layers removed and cut into ¼-inch pieces

1 green bell pepper, seeded and cut into large chunks

1 large shallot, chopped

4 cloves garlic

3 tablespoons peeled and roughly chopped fresh ginger or galangal

3 fresh or frozen Thai lime (makrut) leaves

¼ teaspoon kosher salt

1 teaspoon organic sugar

1–2 serrano chiles, seeded (optional)

FOR THE BROTH

Reserved ¼ cup curry paste (above)

1 can (14 oz) Aroy-D full-fat coconut milk

1 cup water

1 teaspoon Better Than Bouillon no chicken base

1 tablespoon No-Fish Sauce (page 161)

2 tablespoons fresh lime juice

To make the curry paste, begin by toasting the spices. Heat a dry sauté pan over high heat until smoking hot, about 2 minutes. Remove the pan from the heat, tilt it 45 degrees away from your face, add the coriander and cumin, and toss them continuously for 20 to 30 seconds by constantly moving the pan forward in a scooping motion. Never stop moving the pan, or the spices will burn. When the spices are ready, pour them into a food processor. Add the turmeric, lemongrass, bell pepper, shallot, garlic, ginger, lime leaves, salt, sugar, and the chile(s) to taste, if using, and process until smooth. Scoop out ¼ cup of the paste and set it aside for the broth. Transfer the leftover paste to an airtight container and refrigerate for up to 1 week or freeze for up to 1 month.

To make the broth, have your 5 vegetable add-ins ready to go. In a small stockpot, sauté the ¼ cup curry paste over medium heat until fragrant, about 2 minutes. Add the coconut milk, water, and stock base and stir well. Raise the heat to high, add your 5 add-ins, and bring to a boil. Reduce the heat to a simmer and simmer just until the vegetables are tender, about 5 minutes. Adjust the seasoning to taste.

Remove the curry from the heat and stir in the fish sauce and lime juice. Ladle into bowls, garnish with the basil and cilantro, dividing them evenly, and serve with the lime wedges and sticky rice on the side.

FOR THE VEGETABLE ADD-INS (CHOOSE 5)

1 cup cubed firm tofu, in ½-inch cubes

1 cup julienned red onion, in ½-inch-wide julienne

1 cup cut-up Chinese eggplant, in 1-inch pieces

1 cup cut-up red bell pepper, in 1-inch pieces

1 cup sliced carrot, in 1-inch-thick rounds

1 cup cut-up zucchini, in 1-inch pieces

1 cup cut-up asparagus, green beans, or long beans, in 1-inch pieces

1 cup cut-up Chinese broccoli or regular broccoli, in 1-inch pieces

FOR GARNISH

¼ cup loosely packed fresh Thai basil leaves

¼ cup loosely packed fresh cilantro leaves

1 lime, cut into wedges

DAL WITH MINT, THAI LIME & CRUNCHY CHICKPEAS

This dish wraps you in a warm blanket of fragrant spices, creamy protein-packed legumes, and coconut milk—all with the ethereal herbaceous lift of Thai lime leaves and the welcome crunch of roasted chickpeas. In the midst of a busy workday, a cup of this dal over rice will stick to your bones without weighing you down. That said, it's also amazing when you want a warming meal on a lazy weekend. Our masala paste is tried and true, but if you are short on time, pick up a premade masala paste at an Indian grocery or a well-stocked supermarket.

 THE PLAN: While the lentils are soaking, make the masala paste. Then cook the dal and ready the garnishes.

In a bowl, combine the lentils with water to cover and soak for at least 1 hour. If you're a planner, soak them overnight at room temperature for an even creamier, easier-to-digest dal.

Meanwhile, make the masala paste. Heat a small sauté pan over medium heat, add the cumin and coriander seeds, and toast, stirring constantly, until fragrant, about 1 minute. Transfer the spices to a mortar or spice grinder and grind to a powder. (You can also use the flat side of a chef's knife to crush and scrape them into a powder, but it takes a little more elbow grease.) Tip the spice powder into a small food processor, add the ginger, paprika, garam masala, salt, and pepper flakes, and pulse until all the ingredients are incorporated into an even consistency. Add the coconut oil, tomato paste, and cilantro stems and process on high speed for a few minutes until a smooth paste forms. Set aside.

Now, begin to make the sauce for the dal. Heat a large frying pan with a domed lid over medium heat. When the pan is hot, add the oil and onion and cook, stirring often, until the onion is translucent, 4–5 minutes. Add the garlic and cook, stirring, for 1 minute longer. Stir in 3 tablespoons of the masala paste and cook, stirring to prevent scorching, for 1 to 2 minutes. Add the tomatoes and juice, coconut milk, and lime leaves and stir well. Taste the sauce. If it needs more spice from the paste, add another tablespoon (or three!)

Drain the lentils. Raise the heat under the sauce to medium-high and bring the sauce to a boil, stirring occasionally. Add the lentils, reduce the heat to medium-low, and cook, giving the mixture a stir every now and again, until the lentils are tender, 20–25 minutes.

Remove from the heat, fold in the spinach, and season with salt. Divide the dal evenly between individual bowls. Garnish the bowls with the mint, cilantro, sour cream, chickpeas, and lemon wedges, dividing them evenly, and serve.

A DIFFERENT KIND OF MAGIC: Beans get a bad rap because they can cause intestinal gas. But yellow split lentils, or mung dal, are in a class by themselves. Most beans break down in the intestines, which causes bloating. But because of differences in their starch and fiber content, yellow split lentils break down in your stomach, creating much smoother digestion. They're also the most alkaline of all beans, and according to Ayurvedic medicine, they boost immunity and have a calming, grounding effect on the body. We usually order our mung dal online, though Indian shops and some health-food stores carry them.

1½ cups mung dal (yellow split lentils)

FOR THE MASALA PASTE

1½ teaspoons cumin seeds

1½ teaspoons coriander seeds

1-inch piece fresh ginger, peeled and thinly sliced

1 tablespoon smoked paprika

2 teaspoons garam marsala

1 teaspoon kosher salt

1 teaspoon red pepper flakes

2 tablespoons coconut oil, melted

2 tablespoons tomato paste

2 tablespoons fresh cilantro stems

FOR THE SAUCE

1 tablespoon coconut oil

1 small red onion, finely chopped (about 1 cup)

3 large cloves garlic, finely chopped

1 cup canned diced fire-roasted tomatoes with juice

1 can (14 oz) Aroy-D full fat coconut milk

3 fresh or frozen Thai lime (makrut) leaves

2 cups packed spinach leaves, preferably Bloomsdale

Kosher salt

FOR GARNISH

¼ cup loosely packed stemmed fresh mint leaves, torn into ½-inch pieces

3–5 fresh cilantro sprigs, torn into ½-inch pieces

½ cup Tofutti sour cream

¼ cup Crunchy Chickpeas (page 165)

½ lemon, halved

ORECCHIETTE WITH SAUSAGE & BROCCOLINI

Broccolini and spicy sausage make for one of our all-time favorite pasta combinations, and we keep coming back to orecchiette as the best pasta shape for this recipe. If you can find fresh orecchiette, buy it (Blair likes the fancy brands in the refrigerated section), though dried is fine too. If you cannot find broccolini, try broccoli rabe or a combination of regular broccoli and a leafy green like kale or mustard greens. If you want to take this dish to the next level, smoke the sausage on a smoker and/or add Miyoko's winter truffle cheese or Truffle Butter (page 160) to the finished dish.

 THE PLAN: Prep each ingredient in this recipe separately and set aside as you go. This will create the cleanest flavor in the finished dish.

The broccolini and sausages can be cooked on a grill or the stove top. We recommend grilling because it deepens their flavor. Charred bits on the broccolini are especially helpful in bringing the dish together.

To cook on the grill, prepare the grill for direct cooking over medium-high heat. Toss the broccolini with 1 tablespoon of the oil and a pinch of salt. Place the broccolini perpendicular to the bars of the grill rack directly over the fire and grill, flipping once, until you see some browning on both sides, 1–2 minutes on each side. The broccolini will cook again in the sauce, so it does not have to be tender all the way through now. Arrange the sausages directly over the fire and grill, turning as needed, until there is significant caramelization on every side, about 3 minutes on each side. Let the sausages rest for a few minutes while you cut the broccolini into 2-inch lengths, then slice the sausages into ½-inch-thick rounds.

To cook on the stove top, cut the broccolini into 2-inch lengths and the sausages into ½-inch-thick rounds. Put two sauté pans on the stove top over medium-high heat and add 1 tablespoon of the oil to each pan. When the oil is hot, add the broccolini to one pan and the sausages to the other and cook, without turning, until nice and dark brown on the underside (to create depth of flavor), about 5 minutes. Transfer them to a large plate.

While the broccolini and sausages are cooking, fill a large pot three-fourths full with water, bring to a boil over high heat, and then salt the water (see Note). Add the pasta and cook until just shy of al dente, according to the package directions. (It will cook longer in the sauce.) Drain in a colander, toss with 1 tablespoon of the oil, and then spread out on a platter or sheet pan to cool.

Heat a large sauté pan over medium heat. Add the remaining 1 tablespoon oil, the garlic, and pepper flakes (if using) and cook, stirring occasionally, for about 30 seconds. Add the sausages and broccolini, let cook for another 30 seconds, and then add the pasta, butter, and stock. Raise the heat to high and reduce the stock by one-third as it emulsifies with the butter. Add the basil, lemon zest, and half of the Parmesan and toss to mix well.

Transfer to a shallow serving bowl, making sure some of the sauce is visible on top. Garnish with the remaining Parmesan and dig in.

1 bunch broccolini, trimmed

3–4 tablespoons extra-virgin olive oil

Kosher salt

3 Beyond Sausage spicy Italian sausages

1 lb orecchiette, preferably fresh

2 tablespoons finely chopped garlic

1½ teaspoons red pepper flakes (optional)

4 tablespoons Miyoko's unsalted butter

1 cup Better Than Bouillon no chicken stock

¼ cup loosely packed stemmed fresh basil leaves, torn into ½-inch pieces

Grated zest of 1 lemon

½ cup grated plant-based Parmesan cheese, preferably Violife brand (see Note, page 32)

NOTE: Salt the water for cooking pasta until it tastes salty, like seawater. Sometimes people add olive oil to the water, which is a waste of the oil. But after you cook the pasta, you can toss it with a little oil to prevent it from sticking together.

SPRING RISOTTO WITH CORDYCEPS

This seasonal dish calls for cordyceps, an umami-rich fungus with a pleasant earthy flavor. It's long been prescribed in traditional Chinese medicine for everything from improving heart health and memory to slowing aging and is now popular among professional athletes as an endurance booster. While wild cordyceps grows like a parasite on certain insects and spiders, most cultivated versions are vegan, living on brown rice. Dehydrated vegan cordyceps are available online, but the fresh fungus is more difficult to find. If you live in the San Francisco Bay Area, Far West Fungi is a reliable source.

If you want to skip the cordyceps, you won't break the flavor profile of the dish. If omitting them, use 2 cups of oyster mushrooms, which lend their rich, slightly nutty flavor year-round. The asparagus used here shines in the springtime, but you can swap in fresh corn kernels or baby arugula in summer or shredded Swiss chard in winter.

 THE PLAN: Have all the ingredients cut, cooked, or otherwise prepared and the stock at a bare simmer on the stove top before you begin cooking the rice.

Pour the stock into a saucepan, bring to a simmer over medium heat, and then reduce the heat to low. You'll add the stock to the rice slowly, allowing it to absorb and evaporate as the risotto cooks, and keeping it warm helps it to incorporate more evenly.

Place a heavy-bottomed saucepan over high heat and add 1 tablespoon of the butter. When the butter melts and begins to brown, add the oyster mushrooms and a generous pinch of salt. The salt helps the mushrooms to expel water, speeding up the caramelization process. Brown the mushrooms to your preference. Blair likes to cook them dark on one side only to create a contrast in flavor. Transfer the mushrooms to a bowl and set aside.

Wipe the pan clean, using a little water if needed to loosen any stuck bits that can cause the rice to stick. Return the pan to medium-low heat and add 2 tablespoons of the butter, the onion, and the rice. Cook, stirring occasionally, until the onion begins to brown and the rice is ever-so-lightly toasted, 3–5 minutes. Stir in the garlic and thyme, wait for about 1 minute, and then add the Madeira. Cook, stirring occasionally, until the wine reduces by about three-fourths. Add 1 cup of the hot stock, reduce the heat to low, and continue to stir periodically. Blair likes to use low heat because it allows him to do other things while the rice is cooking. If you want to stand over the pot the whole time, you can cook over medium-high heat and stir almost constantly. The stirring is critical either way. It keeps the risotto from sticking to the bottom of the pan, and it causes the rice to shed tiny pieces that break down and create the signature "creamy" risotto consistency.

Once the rice has absorbed the first cup of stock, repeat the process with a second cup. Add a final cup of stock, let the rice absorb it as before, then stir in the mushrooms, asparagus, cordyceps, kale, half the Parmesan, the lemon zest, and the remaining 1 tablespoon unsalted butter or the truffle butter. Remove from the heat, cover, and let rest for 5 minutes.

Spoon the risotto into individual serving bowls, garnish with the remaining Parmesan, and serve.

3 cups Better Than Bouillon no chicken stock

3–4 tablespoons Miyoko's unsalted butter

1 cup cut-up oyster mushrooms, in 1-inch pieces

Kosher salt

½ cup finely diced yellow onion

1 cup Carnaroli or Arborio rice

4 cloves garlic, crushed, then minced

2 tablespoons stemmed fresh thyme leaves (from about 6 sprigs)

½ cup Madeira (see Note)

2 cups diced asparagus, in 1-inch dice

1 cup fresh cordyceps, or ½ cup dried cordyceps rehydrated in hot water

2 cups loosely packed baby kale

½ cup grated plant-based Parmesan cheese, preferably Violife brand (see Note, page 32)

Grated zest of 1 lemon

1 tablespoon Truffle Butter (page 160), optional

NOTE: Madeira is a classic pairing with mushrooms, but dry white wine or sherry can be substituted in a pinch.

PURPLE GNOCCHI
WITH LEMON & ASPARAGUS

We love the colors of this dish, but if you cannot find purple potatoes at your grocery store, Yukon gold potatoes work just fine. We're guiding you through a favorite combination here, but you can also sauce the gnocchi with marinara or melted butter for a quicker preparation.

If you are intimidated by the idea of making gnocchi, we've got your back here, and they are actually the easiest pasta to make. Ideally, you have a potato ricer, which creates a more pillowy finished product. If you don't already have one, consider picking one up.

THE PLAN: Much of the time in this recipe goes toward roasting and cooling the potatoes. You can prepare the sauce and vegetables while that's going on. Then shape the gnocchi, cook them in boiling water, and finish them off in a pan with the other ingredients.

To begin making the gnocchi, preheat the oven to 425°F. Prick each potato in a few spots with a fork so steam can escape during baking. Spread the potatoes in a single layer on a sheet pan and bake until they give easily when pierced with a fork, 30-60 minutes, depending on their size. Let cool.

While the potatoes are roasting and cooling, make the sauce. In a small saucepan, combine the stock, garlic, shallot, thyme, and tarragon and bring to a simmer over medium heat. Simmer uncovered to allow the stock to reduce and build flavor. Meanwhile, in a small bowl, stir together the cornstarch and lemon juice. When the stock has reduced by half, briefly stir the cornstarch mixture to recombine, then whisk it into the stock mixture along with the lemon zest and with the butter pieces in two batches. Raise the heat to medium-high and continue to whisk until the mixture begins to thicken to the consistency of heavy cream, 1-2 minutes. Remove from the heat, strain through a fine-mesh sieve, and return the strained sauce to the pan. Season to taste with salt. Cover the pan and place it at the back of the stove to keep the sauce warm.

Now return to the cooled potatoes. Pass the potatoes through a ricer or use a rubber spatula to push them through a coarse-mesh sieve into a large bowl. Lightly dust a cutting board and a sheet pan with flour. Add the flour, salt, and oil to the potatoes and, using your hands, mix together all the ingredients until evenly distributed, then squeeze the mixture to knead it into a cohesive ball. If the mixture is too sticky, add more flour, a little at a time, until the dough no longer sticks to your hands. If the potatoes will not fully absorb the flour, add a little more oil until the dough comes together.

Transfer the dough to a pastry bag or large resealable plastic bag and twist the top closed. Fitting the pastry bag with a ½-inch round tip is helpful but not necessary. If using a plastic bag, cut a ½-inch hole in a bottom corner. Then, applying gentle pressure at the top of the bag, squeeze out long lines of dough onto the flour-dusted cutting board as if making straight snakes out of Play-Doh. Cut the snakes crosswise into 2-inch-long pieces and transfer them to the prepared sheet pan. If cooking within the next hour, leave at room temperature. If not, put the sheet pan into the freezer until the gnocchi are frozen solid, then transfer them to a resealable plastic bag and store in the freezer until ready to serve (see Note).

Continued on page 50...

FOR THE GNOCCHI

4 lb purple potatoes

2 cups "00" flour, plus more if needed and for dusting

1 tablespoon kosher salt, plus more for cooking

2 tablespoons extra-virgin olive oil, plus more as needed

FOR THE SAUCE

2 cups Better Than Bouillon no chicken stock

3 cloves garlic, smashed with the back of a knife

2 tablespoons thinly sliced shallot

4 fresh thyme sprigs

8 fresh tarragon sprigs

1½ teaspoons cornstarch

Juice of ½ lemon

Grated zest of 1 lemon

½ cup Miyoko's unsalted butter, cut into 1-inch pieces

Kosher salt

FOR THE VEGETABLES

2 tablespoons extra-virgin olive oil

1 small zucchini, halved lengthwise, then cut crosswise into half-moons (1 cup)

Kosher salt

1 cup small broccoli florets or cut-up asparagus, in 2-inch pieces

1 cup packed stemmed torn Swiss chard leaves, in roughly 2-inch squares

TO FINISH AND GARNISH

2 teaspoons extra-virgin olive oil

3 tablespoons grated plant-based Parmesan cheese, preferably Violife brand (see Note, page 32)

1 tablespoon stemmed fresh tarragon leaves, torn into small pieces

Drizzle a little oil on a sheet pan and place near the stove. Fill a large pot three-fourths full with water, bring to a boil over high heat and then salt the water (see Note, page 46. Add half of the gnocchi to the boiling water and cook until they float to the top, about 2 minutes, then cook for 1 minute longer. Using a slotted spoon, transfer the gnocchi to the prepared sheet pan. Repeat with the remaining gnocchi.

Now cook the vegetables. Line a large plate with paper towels. Heat a sauté pan over high heat for about 2 minutes, then add 1 tablespoon of the oil. When you see the smallest amount of smoke rising from the oil, add the zucchini, season with salt, and sear until the underside turns a bit brown, about 1½ minutes. Remove from the heat and transfer the zucchini to the prepared plate to drain and cool. Return the pan to high heat and add the remaining 1 tablespoon oil. When you see the smallest amount of smoke rising from the oil, add the broccoli, reduce the heat to medium, cover the pan, and cook until the underside turns dark brown, 3-4 minutes. Transfer the broccoli to the plate with the zucchini to drain.

To finish the dish, place a nonstick sauté pan over high heat. When the pan is hot, add 1 teaspoon of the oil. Reduce the heat to medium, add half of the gnocchi in a single layer, and sear, turning once, until browned on both sides, about 2 minutes on each side. Transfer to a plate. Repeat with the remaining oil and gnocchi.

Return the pan to medium heat, and half of the chard, broccoli, and zucchini, and heat through. Add half of the gnocchi and then add just enough of the sauce to coat all the ingredients. Toss to coat and warm through. Spoon the gnocchi and vegetables onto the center of an individual serving plate. Repeat with the remaining vegetables, gnocchi, and enough sauce to coat and spoon onto a second serving plate.

Add additional warm sauce to each plate if desired. Garnish with the Parmesan and tarragon, dividing them evenly, and serve.

NOTE: Consider doubling the gnocchi recipe and keeping the extra batch in the freezer for another meal. Every restaurant Blair has worked in has kept gnocchi in the freezer until it's needed. The gnocchi will keep well for up to 1 month. You throw it straight from the freezer into boiling water and you are ready to go!

SAUCY TAHINI-AVOCADO RICE BOWLS

People are eating more food in bowls than ever before. In 2015, *New York* magazine declared bowls to be "the meal of the moment." But here's the thing: the moment never really ended. Today, mounds of rice, vegetables, and proteins inspired by nearly every culture around the globe continue to dominate people's social media feeds and meals.

But there's an art to creating one that doesn't look or taste haphazard. Here's the trick: You'll want vegetables, proteins like legumes or tofu, and whole grains to fill it out. To make it sing, add something crunchy, something creamy, and something fermented or pickled. Finally, a squeeze of citrus can pull everything together even when it's not quite there yet (or three days old).

Here, we're sharing a bowl recipe we make whenever the stars align. Feel free to use what you've got on hand if a substitution makes sense to you, such as swapping out the rice for a sprouted grain mix.

THE PLAN: Prepare all the vegetables in the ingredients list or assemble similar ingredients that you have on hand in your refrigerator. Cook the rice or use any leftover grain in your refrigerator. Make the sauces. Then assemble the bowls and serve.

To make the tahini sauce, in a bowl, stir together all the ingredients, mixing well. You will have more sauce than you need for the bowl. Store the leftover sauce in an airtight container in the refrigerator for up to 1 week.

To make the soy-mirin-maple sauce, stir together all the ingredients in a bowl, mixing well. You will have more sauce than you need for the bowl. Store the leftover sauce in an airtight container in the refrigerator for up to 1 week.

Fill a saucepan about two-thirds full with water and bring to a boil over high heat. Fill a bowl with ice and water and set it near the stove. Add the kale to the boiling water and blanch until soft and bright green, about 1 minute. Drain and immerse in the ice water to stop the cooking. When the kale is completely cool, drain and pat dry.

In a small bowl, mix the kale with just enough of the tahini sauce to coat lightly.

To assemble the bowls, brush the bottom of each bowl with some of the soy-mirin-maple sauce. Use enough of the sauce so it will be visible after you have added the rice. Mound ½ cup of the rice in the center of each bowl. Pepper the vegetables—kale, mushrooms, sweet potato, avocado, kimchi, pickled carrots—in little mounds on top of the rice. For extra visual appeal, try not to put similarly colored ingredients next to one another.

Drizzle both sauces over each bowl: Dip a fork into the soy-mirin-maple sauce, then, holding it about 6 inches above a bowl, move it back and forth in a zigzag pattern to create a drizzle effect. Repeat to dress the second bowl. Then, rinse the fork and use the same method to drizzle the tahini sauce over both bowls. Sprinkle the sesame seeds over each bowl and serve.

FOR THE TAHINI SAUCE
1 cup Just Mayo
¼ cup Joyva tahini
2 ½ tablespoons fresh lemon juice
2 ½ tablespoons soy sauce
Pinch of kosher salt

FOR THE SOY-MIRIN-MAPLE SAUCE
1 cup mirin
½ cup soy sauce
1 tablespoon pure maple syrup
½ teaspoon peeled and grated fresh ginger
1 clove garlic, finely minced to a paste
Kosher salt and freshly ground black pepper

FOR THE BOWLS
2 cups chopped kale or Swiss chard, stems removed
2 cups cooked rice, hot
1 lb mushrooms, any kind, brushed clean, trimmed, sliced, and grilled or sautéed
1 cup roasted and cubed sweet potato, in ½-inch cubes
1 avocado, halved, pitted, peeled, and cut into ½-inch triangles
1 cup store-bought kimchi, such as cabbage, cucumber, or radish
½ cup Quick-Pickled Carrots (page 154)
1 tablespoon toasted sesame seeds

SUMMER TOMATO-BREAD SALAD WITH RICOTTA WHIP & SMOKED TOFU

This bright and filling main-course includes plenty of fresh fruits and vegetables, delicious croutons, and tasty protein to satisfy completely. The recipe is slightly quirky because it requires three different sauces, but they all come together quickly. Although you will use a lot of bowls to make this, the end result is worth. This is one of Blair's most amazingly flavorful salads—trust me.

 THE PLAN: Make the croutons first. Next, make all three sauces. Cut the fruits and vegetables, then sear the tofu, assemble, and serve.

To make the croutons, preheat the oven to 325°F. Line a sheet pan with parchment paper. In a bowl, toss the bread with the oil, then spread the bread on the prepared pan. Toast the bread, rotating the pan from back to front and stirring the croutons halfway through baking, until golden and crunchy, about 20 minutes.

To make the bread sauce, in a blender, combine all the ingredients and blend until smooth. You should have about 1 cup. Set aside.

To make the vinaigrette, in a small bowl, whisk together the vinegar, lemon juice, mustard, and salt, mixing well. Then whisk in the oil until emulsified. You should have about 1/4 cup. Set aside.

To make the ricotta whip, in another small bowl, stir together all the ingredients, mixing well. You should have about ½ cup. Set aside.

Pat the tofu dry with a paper towel. In a sauté pan, heat the oil over medium heat. When the oil is hot, add the tofu and sear, turning as needed, until golden brown on all sides, about 4 minutes on each side.

To assemble the salad, in a bowl, toss the croutons with the bread sauce, coating evenly. Cut the tofu into ½-inch cubes. Have ready two individual serving bowls. Spoon half of the ricotta whip into the center of each bowl. If you want to add a cheffy touch, use the back of the spoon to push the ricotta up the sides of the bowl. In a large bowl, combine the tomatoes, stone fruits, cucumber, arugula, kale, onion, fennel, shiso, and soaked croutons. Drizzle with the vinaigrette and toss to coat evenly.

Divide the salad evenly between the individual bowls, placing it on top of the ricotta. Top with the tofu cubes, dividing them evenly, and serve.

FOR THE CROUTONS

3 cups torn or cut rustic bread chunks, in 1-inch pieces

2 tablespoons extra-virgin olive oil

FOR THE BREAD SAUCE

1 cup chopped tomatoes

2 tablespoons extra-virgin olive oil

1 clove garlic

¼ teaspoon grated lemon zest

1 tablespoon Sriracha sauce

¼ teaspoon kosher salt

FOR THE VINAIGRETTE

1 tablespoon sherry vinegar or red wine vinegar

1 tablespoon fresh lemon juice

2 teaspoons whole-grain mustard

½ teaspoon kosher salt

2 tablespoons extra-virgin olive oil

FOR THE RICOTTA WHIP

½ cup plant-based ricotta cheese, preferably Miyoko's brand

1–2 tablespoons soy milk

Pinch of kosher salt

1 package (8 oz) smoked

1 tablespoon extra-virgin olive oil

1 cup cut-up heirloom tomatoes, in roughly 1-inch pieces

1 cup cut-up stone fruits in 1-inch pieces

About ½ Japanese cucumber, smashed lightly and cut into ½-inch pieces (1 cup)

1 cup packed arugula leaves

1 cup packed baby kale

¼ cup thinly shaved red onion

¼ cup thinly shaved fennel

4 fresh shiso leaves, torn into 1-inch pieces

BALLS OF GOODNESS WITH SORTA-TIKKA SAUCE & PICKLED CARROTS

When I read a menu, I immediately scan it for "balls of goodness." Back in my I'll-eat-anything-you-throw-at-me days, "fried balls of goodness" meant arancini, salt cod fritters, falafel, and meatballs—always meatballs. Even though ground beef has permanently exited my diet, I still crave the crunchy exterior and soft, fluffy middle of a meatball. Thanks to lots of trial and error on Blair's part, these beauties deliver on two levels: the texture is spot-on and they are a complete protein.

A few things about these balls: We like green or black lentils because the end product resembles an actual beef ball. If you don't care about the appearance, go ahead and use red, yellow, or any lentils you like. Black cardamom is exposed to fire during drying, which adds a smoky depth to this dish. If you can find only green cardamom, it is fine to use it instead. Finally, the sorta-tikka sauce is our butter- and cream-free version of tikka masala sauce. It's not much like the original, but it *is* damn delicious.

THE PLAN: Cook the grains first. Next, make and bake the lentil-rice balls. Then make the masala sauce while the balls are baking. Note that Blair likes to fry the balls before eating them. I prefer to eat them baked. You do you.

Cook the rice and quinoa separately according to package directions. You will have 3 cups rice and 2 cups quinoa. Reserve 1 cup of the rice for the balls. Mix together the remaining rice and the quinoa, season with salt, and hold them at a warm temperature until ready to serve.

To make the balls, preheat the oven to 350°F. In a sauté pan, heat the oil over medium heat. Add the onion and cook, stirring occasionally, until translucent, 3–5 minutes. Add the rice and mix evenly with the onion.

Transfer the contents of the pan to a food processor and add the lentils, tomato paste, tamari, nutritional yeast, garlic, egg replacer, miso, oregano, and salt. Pulse until everything is incorporated evenly into a chunky consistency. You do not want a paste. (You may need to do this in two batches, depending on the size of your processor.)

Line a sheet pan with parchment paper. Using a spoon or a small ice-cream scoop, form the mixture into same-size balls and set them, evenly spaced, on the sheet pan. You should have 24 balls. We use a 1-inch ice-cream scoop to make balls about 1 inch in diameter. If you make larger balls, increase the baking time as needed.

Bake the balls until firm and browned on the outside, about 30 minutes.

While the balls are baking, make the sauce. In a saucepan, heat 2 tablespoons of the oil over medium-low heat. Add the onion, ginger, turmeric, and garlic and cook, stirring occasionally, until the onion is translucent, about 10 minutes. Add the tomato paste, cardamom, paprika, coriander, cumin, garam masala, salt, pepper flakes, and the remaining 2 tablespoons oil, stir well, and cook, stirring occasionally, until fragrant, about 2 minutes.

Add the tomatoes and juice, coconut cream, cashews, stock base, and water and mix well. Reduce the heat to low, cover, and simmer until the flavors come together and the sauce just begins to thicken, 10–15 minutes. Add the lemon zest and juice. Taste and adjust the seasoning if needed. Remove from the heat and let cool for a few minutes.

FOR THE GRAINS

1 cup brown or jasmine rice

¾ cup quinoa, well rinsed

Kosher salt

FOR THE LENTIL-RICE BALLS

2 tablespoons extra-virgin olive oil

¼ cup finely chopped yellow onion

1 cup cooked brown rice (above)

2 cups drained cooked green or black lentils

¼ cup tomato paste

¼ cup tamari

2 tablespoons nutritional yeast

1 tablespoon minced garlic

1 tablespoon Bob's Red Mill Egg Replacer, prepared for 1 whole egg according to package directions

1 tablespoon white (shiro) miso

1 teaspoon dried oregano

Generous pinch of kosher salt

FOR THE SORTA-TIKKA SAUCE

4 tablespoons extra-virgin olive oil

1 cup coarsely diced red onion

3 tablespoons peeled and sliced fresh ginger

2 tablespoons peeled and sliced fresh turmeric

2 tablespoons roughly chopped garlic (3–4 large cloves)

Transfer the sauce to a blender and blend until smooth. If you prefer a thinner consistency, blend in a few spoonfuls of water. Keep warm until ready to serve (or reheat as needed). You will need only 1 cup of the sauce for this recipe. The leftover sauce will keep in an airtight container in the refrigerator for up to 1 week.

You can eat the balls straight from the oven or you can deep-fry or sear them for added flavor. To deep-fry them, line a large platter with paper towels and set it near the stove. Pour the vegetable oil to a depth of about 3 inches into a deep, heavy pot and heat to 350°F on a deep-frying thermometer (see Note, page 70). Working in batches to avoid crowding, carefully lower the balls into the hot oil and fry until crisp on the outside and warm at the center, 2–3 minutes. Using a slotted spoon, transfer the balls to the paper-lined platter to drain. Repeat until all the balls are fried.

To sear the balls, in a large sauté pan, heat the olive oil over medium heat. Working in batches to avoid crowding, add the balls to the pan and sear, turning as needed, until browned on all sides, about 5 minutes. Transfer to a platter and repeat until all the balls are seared.

To plate, place 1 cup of the warm mixed grains in the bottom of each individual serving bowl. Arrange 6 balls to one side of the grains and top the balls with about ¼ cup of the tikka sauce. Spoon about ¼ cup of the white sauce over the other half of the grains, top with the pickled carrots, herb sprigs, and a lemon wedge, and serve.

NOTE: To save time, you can buy tikka masala paste and just add liquid, pickled carrots (or other pickled vegetables), and/or an herb-forward sour cream- or yogurt-based white sauce. If you opt for purchased sauces, the recipe will no longer be vegan, of course, but the result will still be satisfying.

2 tablespoons tomato paste

1–2 black cardamom pods

2 tablespoons smoked paprika

1 tablespoon ground coriander

1 tablespoon ground cumin

1 ½ teaspoons garam masala

½ teaspoon kosher salt

½ teaspoon red pepper flakes

1 ½ cups canned diced fire-roasted tomatoes with juice

1 can (14 oz) Aroy-D coconut cream or full-fat coconut milk

½ cup roasted cashews

1 teaspoon Better Than Bouillon no chicken base

½ cup water

Grated zest and juice of 1 lemon

Vegetable oil or rice bran for deep-frying (optional)

2 tablespoons olive oil for searing (optional)

1 cup Mint-Garlic White Sauce (page 155)

Quick-Pickled Carrots (page 154) for serving

Fresh mint or cilantro sprigs for garnish

1 lemon, cut into 4 wedges

VEGETABLE PAELLA WITH SAFFRON & SAUSAGE

The restaurant version of this dish has been a best-seller at Wildseed since day one. Creating a plant-based version of iconic paella calls for plenty of innovation. Rice is vegan, but we shy away from meals that rely too heavily on carbs, so our take on paella has a mixture of grains to diversify the nutrient profile and is heavy on vegetables.

 THE PLAN: Make the sofrito and rouille first. Next, precook the grains and cut all the vegetables. Then build the paella, cook on the stove top, and finish under the broiler.

To make the sofrito, select a heavy-bottomed pan about 14 inches in diameter (this is the same pan in which you will cook the paella), place over medium heat, and add the oil. When the oil sizzles, add the onions, bell pepper, garlic, and salt and cook, stirring occasionally, until the vegetables begin to show some color, 5–10 minutes. Pour in the wine and deglaze the pan, dislodging any browned bits on the pan bottom, then simmer until the wine reduces by half.

Stir in the tomato paste and continue to cook, stirring occasionally, until the pan is relatively dry. Stir in the paprika and saffron, remove from the heat, and let cool to room temperature.

To make the rouille, in a microwave-safe bowl, combine the lemon zest and juice, garlic, salt, and saffron and microwave for 30 seconds. Let cool to room temperature, then fold into the mayonnaise. Cover and refrigerate until needed.

To cook the grains, in a small saucepan, mix together the quinoa, millet, and buckwheat and cook according to the package directions, stopping the cooking when the grains are half cooked. Cook the rice in a separate small saucepan according to the package directions, stopping when the rice is half cooked. Combine the mixed grains and rice and let cool. You will need only 1½ cups cooked grains; refrigerate the remainder for another use.

While the grains are cooling, prepare the vegetables and sausage. Fill a small saucepan about two-thirds full with water and bring to a boil over high heat. Fill a bowl with ice and water and set it near the stove. Add the cauliflower to the boiling water and blanch for 30 seconds. Drain and immerse in the ice water until cool, then drain and pat dry.

In a sauté pan, heat a splash of oil over medium-high heat. Add the fennel and sear on the underside until browned, about 2 minutes. Transfer to a plate. Wipe out the pan, return it to medium-high heat, and add another splash of oil. Add the sausage slices and sear, without turning, until nice and dark brown on the underside, about 5 minutes. Transfer to the plate with the fennel.

Continued on page 58...

FOR THE SOFRITO

½ cup extra-virgin olive oil

1½ yellow onions, finely diced

½ cup seeded and finely diced bell pepper

1½ cloves garlic, minced

Pinch of kosher salt

½ cup dry white wine

1½ teaspoons tomato paste

1 tablespoon smoked paprika

Pinch of saffron threads

FOR THE ROUILLE

Grated zest and juice of 1 large lemon

½ teaspoon minced garlic

¼ teaspoon kosher salt

Pinch of saffron threads

½ cup Just Mayo

FOR THE MIXED GRAINS

¼ cup quinoa, well rinsed

¼ cup millet

¼ cup buckwheat

½ cup Bomba or Arborio brown rice

⅓ cup cut-up cauliflower, in roughly 1-inch pieces

Extra-virgin olive oil for searing, plus 2 tablespoons

½ cup cut-up fennel, in ⅛-inch wedges

1 cup sliced Beyond Sausage spicy Italian sausage, in ½-inch-thick coins

You need only ½ cup of the sofrito for the paella. Scoop out the excess into an airtight container and refrigerate for another use. Add the 1 ½ cups cooked grain mixture, the remaining 2 tablespoons oil, the salt, and the paprika to the sofrito in the pan, mix well, and then spread the mixture evenly over the bottom of the pan. Place the pan over medium heat. Meanwhile, in a small pan, bring the stock to a boil and position an oven rack in the lower third of the oven and preheat the broiler.

When a crust begins to form on the bottom of the grain mixture, after about 5 minutes, pour in the stock, distributing it evenly, and then remove the pan from the heat. Do not stir the grain mixture. Add the fennel, cauliflower, peppers, sausage, and olives, distributing them evenly throughout the pan and pushing them gently into the grain mixture.

Place the pan at the back of the bottom oven rack and broil until a light crust begins to form on the top and the liquid is reduced by 90 percent, 10–15 minutes.

Garnish the paella with the parsley, lemon, and rouille and serve.

¼ teaspoon kosher salt

¼ teaspoon smoked paprika

1 cup Better Than Bouillon no chicken stock

⅓ cup cut-up Jimmy Nardello peppers, in 1-inch pieces (shishito or baby bell can be substituted)

½ cup Castelvetrano olives

2 tablespoons minced fresh flat-leaf parsley

1 lemon, cut into wedges

NOTE: You can also bake rather than broil the paella for the final step. Position the oven rack in the lower third of the oven as directed and then preheat the oven to 425°F. The timing will be the same.

WARM FARRO WITH CARAMELIZED BROCCOLI, TOFU & CREAMY MISO

This recipe showcases Blair's signature move with broccoli: he sears it until crispy on just one side, then covers the pan to cook it through. This method achieves a layer of caramelized depth without losing the fresh flavor of the vegetable.

Now let's talk about how much we love farro. Maybe it's the nutty flavor. Maybe it's the slightly chewy texture. Maybe it's the fact that it's ten times healthier for you than white rice. Add some crispy kale, golden tofu, Castelvetrano olives, miso sauce, and Blair's signature broccoli move and you've got an unforgettable dish

THE PLAN: Turn on the oven to 300°F and toast the cashews (if you don't already have them on hand), then crank up the oven to 425°F to cook the kale and tofu. Cook the farro. Cut and prepare the other ingredients. Then bake the tofu and kale, make the miso sauce, and cook the broccoli. Assemble and serve.

Preheat the oven to 425°F.

While the oven is heating, put the farro on to cook. In a saucepan, combine the farro, stock, butter, garlic, and salt and bring to a boil over medium-high heat. Reduce the heat to a low, slow boil and cook gently until tender, about 15 minutes. Remove from the heat, cover to keep warm, and set aside.

To prepare the kale and tofu, coarsely grind the coriander in a mortar with a pestle. Transfer to a small bowl, add the oil, Aleppo pepper, and salt and mix well. Pile the kale leaves on a sheet pan, drizzle with half of the spicy oil, and toss to coat the leaves evenly, then spread the leaves in a single layer. Pile the tofu on a second sheet pan, drizzle with the remaining spicy oil, toss to coat the tofu evenly, and then spread the tofu in a single layer. Place both pans in the oven and roast the kale and tofu, stirring them twice and rotating the pans from back to front once during roasting, until the tofu is golden brown and the kale is crispy, about 30 minutes.

To make the sauce, in a bowl, whisk together all the ingredients, mixing well. Set aside.

In a large bowl, toss the broccoli with the oil, coating it evenly. Add the Aleppo pepper and salt and toss again to coat evenly.

Place a sauté pan large enough to hold all the broccoli pieces in a single layer over medium heat. When it is hot, add the broccoli pieces, flat side down, and allow to cook undisturbed until you see the bottoms are getting dark brown and crispy, 3–5 minutes. If the broccoli pieces are not very flat, push down on them with a broad spatula while they are cooking to get an even sear. You don't want to burn the broccoli, but you do want the edges a little crispy. Once the sear is good, cover the pan and cook undisturbed until cooked through, about 2 minutes. Again, try not to move or flip the broccoli.

To assemble the dish, divide the sauce evenly among four individual serving bowls. For a cheffy touch, use the back of a spoon to spread the sauce up the sides of the bowl as if spreading tomato sauce on a pizza crust. Divide the warm farro evenly among the bowls, spooning it either in the center of the bowl or off to one side. (Plating is your chance to be artistic!) In a bowl, toss together the roasted kale and tofu, broccoli, olives, and parsley. Arrange over the farro and sauce. Top with the hemp hearts and cashews and serve.

FOR THE FARRO

1 cup semi-pearled farro

3 cups Better than Bouillon no chicken stock

1 tablespoon Miyoko's unsalted butter

2 cloves garlic, gently crushed with the back of a knife

½ teaspoon kosher salt

FOR THE KALE AND TOFU

2 teaspoons coriander seeds

1 tablespoon extra-virgin olive oil

1 teaspoon Aleppo pepper

½ teaspoon kosher salt

2 cups packed torn stemmed Lacinato kale, in 2-inch pieces

1 package (14 oz) firm or smoked tofu, patted dry and cut into 1-inch cubes

FOR THE SAUCE

¼ cup water

¼ cup fresh lemon juice

2 tablespoons extra-virgin olive oil

2 tablespoons white (shiro) miso

1 tablespoon Joyva tahini

½ teaspoon grated lemon zest

Pinch of kosher salt

1 lb broccoli (about 2 small heads), cut into 2-inch pieces

1 tablespoon extra-virgin olive oil

½ teaspoon Aleppo pepper

½ teaspoon kosher salt

¼ cup Castelvetrano olives, pitted and halved

3 tablespoons fresh large flat-leaf parsley leaves

2 tablespoons hemp hearts

¼ cup cashews, toasted (see Note, page 33)

BARBECUE-GRILLED VEGETABLES & BEYOND SAUSAGE

Barbecue means different things to different people. Being from the South, Blair knows it as meat or vegetables cooked low and slow over a pit or in a smoker. In the Northeast and California, it refers to anything cooked on the grill—even (gasp!) boneless, skinless chicken breasts.

Here's a funny story: In Blair's early catering days, he once fulfilled a "barbecue" order for two hundred people in San Francisco with 100 pounds of Southern barbecue. It was a pool party and when he showed up without an actual grill...let's just say the definition of the word *barbecue* was a sticking point. I'm glad we can laugh about it now!

The method for grilling vegetables and Beyond Sausage that we detail here would have worked much better for that pool party. We listed the vegetables we grill most often, but you can substitute other vegetables if you like.

 THE PLAN: Start the grill. While it's heating up, cut the vegetables, then season them with salt, pepper, and olive oil. Slowly grill. Toss in the sauce and eat.

Prepare the grill for direct cooking over medium-high heat. If using a charcoal grill, try to keep the heat as even as possible. To gauge if the heat is even, quickly move your hand above the grill rack to see if it feels hotter in some spots than others. If it does, lift the rack and reposition the coals as needed. You can use metal or bamboo skewers or a fish or other grilling basket for the vegetables. If using bamboo skewers, soak them in water while the fire heats to prevent them from burning on the grill.

Lightly brush the cauliflower and mushrooms with oil, then season with salt and pepper. Make sure the oil is not dripping from the vegetables, which can cause flare-ups. Thread the vegetables onto skewers or arrange them in a grilling basket. Be sure to leave space between the pieces.

Place the vegetables on the grill directly over the fire and grill, flipping them only once, until caramelized on the outside and tender on the inside. This usually takes about 5 minutes on each side, depending on the intensity of your fire. When they are ready, remove them from the grill.

Arrange the sausages directly over the fire and cook until you see that a crust has formed on the underside, then flip them and grill until a crust forms on the second side. This should take 2-5 minutes on each side, again depending on the intensity of your fire. When they are browned on both sides, transfer them to a plate to rest for 3-4 minutes before serving them.

Remove the vegetables from the skewers or grilling basket and put them into a bowl. Add just enough barbecue sauce to glaze them lightly—about ¼ cup—and toss to coat evenly. Arrange the vegetables and sausages on a platter and serve.

2 cups cauliflower florets and ribs, in 1 ½–1 ¾-inch pieces

½ lb mushrooms, such as oyster, king trumpet, cremini, and/or maitake, in 1 ½–1 ¾-inch pieces

Extra-virgin olive oil for brushing

Kosher salt and freshly ground black pepper

2 Beyond Sausage spicy Italian sausages

Store-bought barbecue sauce of choice (we like Stubb's Hickory Bourbon)

HOT DOGS WITH FUJI APPLE SLAW

This recipe was born while we were visiting friends in Jackson Hole, Wyoming, a mountain paradise not exactly known for its meat-free dining options. We helped our friends host a barbecue at their home, so we made a trip to the market to scoop up whatever plant-based grill-friendly options it had for us. Luckily, some Beyond Sausages were in the freezer case. When guests spotted the plant-based sausages, which look very much like pork sausages, a barrage of questions ensued. What are they made of? How do they taste? Then a bunch of meat eaters gobbled them all down within minutes. That stampede showed us that meat eaters are not only interested in eating less meat but are also willing to try something new with a different flavor profile. Here's the recipe from that fateful night.

THE PLAN: First, get the grill ready. Next, make the slaw. If you can, let the slaw sit for about 30 minutes before eating. Mix the sauce. Throw the sausages onto the grill, followed by the buns for the last 30 seconds. Then assemble and serve.

Prepare the grill for direct cooking over medium-high heat.

To make the slaw, in a bowl, stir and toss together the cabbage, green onion, and apple. In a small bowl, stir together the sour cream, oil, lemon juice, and cilantro, mixing well. Add to the cabbage mixture and stir to mix evenly. Season with salt and pepper, then let sit until ready to use.

To make the sauce, in a small bowl, stir together the mustard and mayonnaise, mixing well. Set aside.

Arrange the sausages directly over the fire and grill, turning as needed, until nicely charred on all sides. This usually takes 3–5 minutes, depending on the intensity of your fire. Toast the buns, cut side down, directly over the fire for about 30 seconds.

To assemble, spread the cut sides of each bun evenly with the sauce, then tuck about ¼ cup kimchi and a sausage into each bun. Top with the slaw and dig in.

A FEW NOTES ABOUT THESE DOGS: This is a recipe to play with! You can add French's fried onions, Sriracha sauce, jalapeños, or shaved red onions to spice it up. If you want to leave off the kimchi, roasted red peppers, pickled vegetables, or plant-based chili makes a great addition. Many commercial mustard brands have a little white wine in them, and you usually cannot know if the wine is vegan. Most whole-grain mustard varieties do not include white wine, so if you are avoiding plant-based products 100 percent of the time, it's safer to seek those out.

FOR THE SLAW

2 cups finely shredded green cabbage

1 large green onion, white and green parts, finely chopped

½ cup julienned Fuji apple

1½ tablespoons Tofutti sour cream

1½ tablespoons extra-virgin olive oil

1 tablespoon fresh lemon juice

2 tablespoons chopped fresh cilantro leaves and stems

Kosher salt and freshly ground black pepper

FOR THE SAUCE

¼ cup whole-grain mustard

¼ cup Just Mayo

FOR THE DOGS

4 plant-based sausages or hot dogs (we like Beyond Sausage spicy Italian)

One 4-pack pretzel sausage buns (we like Pretzilla brand)

1 cup kimchi

SICHUAN MAPO-STYLE TOFU

In 2010, Danny Bowien popularized Sichuan food in San Francisco when he opened Mission Chinese Food. At the time, he wanted to pay homage to a brand of Chinese eating that was spicier than what most Americans were familiar with. I'll never forget my first bite of his take on mapo tofu riddled with Sichuan peppercorns, a floral, citrusy spice that has a numbing effect on the tongue. It's the kind of heat that grinds conversation to a halt and, with each new bite, slowly creeps up on you, demanding a beer. I was a food editor at the time, eating out almost every night, and Danny's mapo tofu was one of the most exciting plates I ate that year.

If you are a plant-based eater who has never tried this heady dish of ground pork and tofu, we're excited to offer a similar dish here. At the time of this writing, neither Beyond Meat nor Impossible Foods has a ground "pork" product on the market, but that is likely to change soon. For now, we offer the option of ground "beef" or, if you are not a fan of plant-based meat, mushrooms.

 THE PLAN: Prepare all the ingredients. Then put the rice on to cook and toast and grind the peppercorns. After that, this dish comes together quickly in one pan.

Cook the rice according to the package directions with one exception: dissolve the stock base in the water before adding the rice.

Heat a wok or sauté pan over medium heat, add the Sichuan peppercorns, and toast, shaking the pan occasionally, until fragrant, about 2 minutes. Transfer to a mortar or spice grinder, let cool, and grind to a powder. Set aside.

In a small bowl, combine the stock, wine, bean paste, soy, and cornstarch and mix well. In a second small bowl, stir together the chile oil and chile crisp (if using). Set both bowls aside.

If using the plant-based ground meat, return the wok or sauté pan to high heat and add the rice bran oil. When the oil is hot, add the meat and cook, stirring, until browned, about 2 minutes. Add the garlic and ginger and cook, stirring, until fragrant, about 30 seconds.

If using the mushrooms, return the wok or sauté pan to medium heat, add the mushrooms to the dry pan, and cook, stirring occasionally, until the edges are caramelized, about 3 minutes. Add the rice bran oil, then the garlic and ginger, and cook, stirring, until the garlic and ginger are fragrant, about 1 minute. (Cooking the mushrooms in a dry pan and then adding the oil ensures the mushrooms won't taste oily in the finished dish.)

Quickly stir the cornstarch mixture to recombine, then add to the pan with the meat or mushrooms. Cook, stirring occasionally, until the sauce boils and thickens, about 2 minutes. Remove from the heat and gently fold in the tofu. Transfer to a serving bowl, spoon the chile oil mixture on top, and sprinkle with the Sichuan peppercorns, green onions, and cilantro. Serve with the rice.

1 cup short-grain brown rice

4 teaspoons Better Than Bouillon no chicken base

1 tablespoon Sichuan peppercorns

¾ cup Better Than Bouillon no chicken stock

3 tablespoons Shaoxing wine or dry sherry

2 tablespoons Sichuan broad bean paste in red chile oil (see Note)

1½ tablespoons light soy sauce

1 teaspoon cornstarch

2 tablespoons roasted chile oil

1 tablespoon Laoganma brand spicy chile crisp (see Note), optional

2 tablespoons rice bran oil

¼ lb ground plant-based meat, or ½ lb button, shiitake, or king trumpet mushrooms, brushed clean and cut into pea-size pieces

1 tablespoon finely minced garlic

1 tablespoon peeled and finely minced fresh ginger

¾ lb silken tofu, cut into 1-inch cubes

¼ cup thinly sliced green onions, white and light green parts

Fresh cilantro sprigs for garnish

NOTE: For the best quality, look for the bean paste and chile crisp in an Asian market. Laoganma brand spicy chile crisp is flat out one of the best spicy condiments on earth. If you are staying away from MSG, the Serious Eats website (www.seriouseats.com) has a great recipe for chile crisp made without MSG.

BAJA-STYLE TOFU TACOS
WITH APPLE-SPROUT SLAW

Tofu is overused in plant-based cooking, but it does have its places. One of those places is cloaked inside a light crunchy batter, hidden underneath some sweet slaw and spicy sauce, and folded into a warm tortilla. Yes, my friends, we're talking about a Baja-style beer-battered tofu taco. It is amazing how closely these battered and fried tofu sticks resemble their traditional fish counterparts. They go great with cold beer.

THE PLAN: Make the slaw. Prep the tofu, then make the aioli. Begin to heat up the oil on the stove top as you mix the dry ingredients for the beer batter and get the wet ingredients ready. Then batter and fry the tofu. Heat up the tortillas. Assemble the tacos and serve.

To make the slaw, in a bowl, mix together the brussels sprouts, apple, onion, and cilantro. In a separate bowl, stir together the sour cream, oil, lemon juice and zest, and salt with a fork. Then add the dressing to the slaw and toss and stir to mix evenly. (It is best to make the slaw first so the flavors can marry. If it can sit for an hour, it's even better.)

Press the tofu between your palms to remove excess moisture, then cut the tofu into 3 x 1 x ½-inch strips. Line a large plate with a double layer of paper towels. Place the tofu strips in a single layer on the towels and cover with a second double layer of paper towels. Then set a second large plate on top to press out additional excess moisture until ready to fry.

To make the aioli, in a small bowl, combine all the ingredients and mix well. Set aside.

To make the batter, in a bowl, stir together 1 cup of the rice flour, the all-purpose flour, the baking powder, and salt. You'll add the beer at the last minute to retain as many bubbles as possible. Spread the remaining 1 cup rice flour on a plate to use for dredging the tofu strips.

Pour the rice bran oil to a depth of about 2 inches into a deep, heavy pot and heat to 375°F on a deep-frying thermometer (see Note, page 70). While the oil heats, roll the tofu strips in the rice flour on the plate, coating evenly and patting off any excess. Set aside.

Add half the beer to the dry batter ingredients, mix well, then add the remaining beer and mix well. Adding the beer in batches helps preserve the carbonation. Also, don't worry about lumps. It is better to have some little lumps than to beat the carbonation out of the batter.

When the oil is ready, line a large plate with paper towels and set it near the stove. Working in batches to avoid crowding, dip some of the dredged tofu strips into the batter, coating evenly and letting the excess drip off, then gently drop the strips into the oil. Fry, turning occasionally with a fish spatula or other slotted spatula, until golden brown, and heated through, 5-7 minutes. Using the spatula, transfer the strips to the towel-lined plate to drain. Repeat with the remaining strips. Keep the tofu strips warm on a sheet pan lined with paper towels or topped with a wire rack in the oven.

Place a small frying pan over medium heat. When the pan is hot, one at a time, place the tortillas in the hot pan and heat, turning once, for about 30 seconds on each side. As the tortillas are ready, stack them on one end of a kitchen towel and cover them with the other to keep warm.

To assemble the tacos, smear each tortilla with a generous amount of the aioli. Top with some tofu, cabbage slaw, 2 avocado slices, and some pickled onions, if using, then fold closed. Serve with the lime wedges.

FOR THE SLAW

½ lb brussels sprouts, thinly shaved on a mandoline

1 cup thin-matchstick-cut apple, such as Fuji or Pink Lady

¼ cup thinly sliced red onion

¼ cup chopped fresh cilantro leaves and stems

2 tablespoons Tofutti sour cream

1 ½ tablespoons extra-virgin olive oil

2 tablespoons fresh lemon or lime juice

1 teaspoon grated lemon or lime zest

½ teaspoon kosher salt

1 package (14 oz) firm tofu

FOR THE AIOLI

½ cup Just Mayo

2 tablespoons fresh lime juice

2 tablespoons roughly chopped canned chipotle chiles in adobo sauce

1 teaspoon Laoganma brand spicy chile crisp (see Note, page 63)

FOR THE BATTER

2 cups fine rice flour

1 cup all-purpose flour

1 teaspoon baking powder

2 teaspoons kosher salt

2 cups beer (lager)

Rice bran oil for deep-frying

12 soft corn tortillas, each 6 inches in diameter

1 avocado, halved, pitted, peeled, and thinly sliced (24 slices)

Pickled Onions (page 154), optional

Lime wedges, for serving

MUSHROOM BOLOGNESE WITH PAPPARDELLE & CHARD

When you want to hunker down on a chilly night, there are few dishes more soul satisfying than pasta with tomatoey, meaty ragù—and we mean "meaty" in the most meat-free way, of course. I minored in Italian in college and spent a lot of time living and working in Italy, so pasta is firmly entrenched in our family's repertoire.

This is an easier-to-make-at-home version of the Wildseed Bolognese pasta, which has been the number-one seller at the restaurant since day one. Here, Blair set out to preserve the rich umami of caramelized animal proteins wrapped around al dente noodles. If you have the time to make or buy fresh pasta, it makes quite a difference.

 THE PLAN: Make the sauce. Blanch the chard. Cook the pasta. Combine, eat, and revel in the comfort.

To make the sauce, preheat the oven to 400°F. While the oven is heating, combine the cremini, shiitake, and porcini (if using) mushrooms in a small heatproof bowl and pour in boiling water just to cover (about 1½ cups). Let stand for 1 hour.

Meanwhile, lightly oil a small sheet pan. Cut the plum tomatoes in half lengthwise and place them, cut side down, on the prepared pan. Roast until they have darkened, about 20 minutes. Let cool for a few minutes and then roughly chop.

Remove the rehydrated mushrooms from their soaking water and reserve the water. Discard the shiitake stems, then dice all the mushrooms. In a pot, heat the oil and 2 tablespoons of the butter over medium heat. Add the meat, onion, celery, carrot, and 1 teaspoon salt (the salt helps the vegetables to "sweat") and cook, stirring, until the vegetables and meat begin to color, about 3 minutes. Pour in the wine and let cook for 3–4 minutes to burn off most of the alcohol. Add the mushrooms, canned tomatoes and juice, roasted tomatoes, sour cream, and nutmeg and stir well. Season with salt, reduce the heat to medium-low, and simmer for 30 minutes to blend the flavors. You will need 2 cups of the sauce for the pasta. The leftover sauce can be stored in an airtight container in the refrigerator for up to 1 week.

While the sauce is simmering, fill a saucepan two-thirds full with water and bring to a boil over high heat. Strip the leaves from the chard stems and tear the leaves into bite-size pieces. (Reserve the stems for another use.) Add the chard to the boiling water, give it a stir, and blanch for 30 seconds. Drain into a colander and immediately rinse under cold

FOR THE SAUCE

2 cups dried cremini mushrooms

½ cup dried shiitake mushrooms

½ cup dried porcini mushrooms (optional)

2 tablespoons extra-virgin olive oil, plus more for the sheet pan

2 plum tomatoes

3 tablespoons Miyoko's unsalted butter

½ lb ground plant-based beef, preferably Impossible or Beyond brand

⅔ cup chopped yellow onion

½ cup chopped celery

⅔ cup peeled and chopped carrot

Kosher salt

1 cup dry white wine

1 can (14 oz) diced San Marzano tomatoes with juice

¼ cup Tofutti sour cream

¼ teaspoon freshly grated nutmeg

½ bunch Swiss chard

1 lb fresh pappardelle

2 tablespoons plant-based ricotta cheese, preferably Miyoko's brand

Grated plant-based Parmesan cheese, preferably Violife brand (see Note, page 32), for garnish

water to stop the cooking. (You want it to retain texture and color now because it cooks again briefly with the sauce and pasta.) Drain well, gently squeeze out any remaining water, and set aside.

Fill a large pot three-fourths full with water, bring to a boil over high heat, and then salt the water (see Note, page 46). While the water is heating, transfer the 2 cups of the sauce to a sauté pan large enough to hold the pasta once it is cooked and warm gently. Add the pasta to the boiling water and cook until al dente, according to the package directions. (Many store-bought fresh pastas instruct you to cook the noodles for too long. Two minutes is often enough for fresh pappardelle.)

Just before the pasta is ready, add the chard to the sauce. Then drain the pasta and immediately add it to the sauce along with the remaining 1 tablespoon butter. Mix well, then transfer to individual serving bowls, top each serving with a dollop of ricotta and a dusting of grated Parmesan, and serve.

A HUMBLE PLUG FOR TRUFFLE BUTTER: By now you've seen us suggest adding truffle butter to a couple of dishes. Many chefs think truffle-flavored products are a little hokey because they bastardize the original. That said, truffle butter—when you make it at home—is unequivocally delicious. If you're up for it, toss this pasta with a tablespoon or two (page 160) before you plate it. Drool.

GENERAL TSO'S MUSHROOMS
WITH TOFU & CHINESE BROCCOLI

There was a time when we almost opened a Chinese-inspired restaurant, rooted in Blair's deep appreciation for Chinese food. Nine times out of ten, Blair is experimenting with Asian flavor profiles in our home kitchen. This particular recipe came out of a desire to turn the Chinese-American icon General Tso's chicken into something we could eat at home within our plant-based diet. Mushrooms fit the bill as a chicken substitute because they are meaty (for lack of a better word) and packed with umami. The tofu creates a nice, velvety contrast. We use Hodo brand tofu for two reasons: we like the flavor and texture and it is vacuum-packed, so no pressing is required. You can swap in your own favorite brand. Finally, if you don't want to fry the ingredients in this dish, you can bake them. Either way, this dish is seriously bursting with flavor and highly addictive.

THE PLAN: Collect, cut, and measure all the ingredients. If you are baking the mushrooms and tofu, preheat the oven. Make the sauce, the wet breading, and the dry breading. Cook your rice and then bread and bake or fry the mushrooms and tofu while you steam the broccoli.

If you plan to bake the mushrooms and tofu, preheat the oven to 375°F.

To make the sauce, in a small bowl, combine the water, soy sauce, wine, vinegar, sesame oil, orange zest, sugar, and cornstarch and mix well, dissolving the sugar and cornstarch.

In a sauté pan, combine the rice bran oil, garlic, ginger, and shallot over medium heat and cook, stirring, until all the ingredients are cooked through but not browned, about 1 minute. Quickly stir the cornstarch mixture to recombine, then add to the pan and cook, stirring occasionally, until the sauce boils and thickens, about 1 minute. Remove from the heat and keep warm.

To make the wet breading, combine all the ingredients in a bowl and mix well. To make the dry breading, combine all the ingredients in a bowl and mix well. Add the mushrooms to the wet breading and stir to coat evenly. Then, with your dominant hand, remove the mushroom pieces one at a time, shaking off the excess liquid, and toss them in the dry breading to coat evenly, again shaking off the excess. (A small colander held over the trash can help with this effort.)

If you are frying the mushrooms and tofu, line a large platter with paper towels and set it near the stove. Pour the rice bran oil to a depth of 1½–2 inches into a deep, heavy pot and heat to 350°F on a deep-frying thermometer (see Note, page 70). Working in small batches to avoid crowding, carefully drop the mushroom pieces into the hot oil and fry until golden brown, about 4 minutes. Using a slotted spoon, transfer the mushrooms to the towel-lined plate to drain. Repeat until all the mushrooms are fried.

Continued on page 70...

FOR THE SAUCE

3 tablespoons water

3 tablespoons light soy sauce or tamari

2 tablespoons Shaoxing wine or dry sherry

2 tablespoons rice vinegar

1½ teaspoons toasted sesame oil

1 teaspoon grated orange zest

3 tablespoons organic sugar

1 tablespoon cornstarch

2 teaspoons rice bran or avocado oil

1½ teaspoons minced garlic

1½ teaspoons peeled and minced fresh ginger

2 teaspoons minced shallot

FOR THE WET BREADING

1 tablespoon Bob's Red Mill Egg Replacer, prepared for 1 whole egg according to package directions

¼ cup water

2 tablespoons light soy sauce or tamari

2 tablespoons Shaoxing wine or dry sherry

2 tablespoons vodka

3 tablespoons cornstarch

¼ teaspoon baking soda

3 tablespoons cornstarch

FOR THE DRY BREADING

½ cup superfine rice flour

½ cup cornstarch

½ teaspoon baking powder

½ teaspoon kosher salt

To fry the tofu, bread and fry the same way and drain on the towel-lined plate.

If you are baking the mushrooms and tofu, line one large sheet pan with parchment paper. Bread the mushrooms and tofu as you would for deep-frying and arrange them in a single layer on the prepared pan. Bake, turning them over halfway through baking, until golden brown, about 25 minutes.

Once you've got the mushrooms and tofu cooking, steam the broccoli until tender, about 3 minutes. Or microwave the broccoli as described in the sidebar. It should still be bright green. If the color is dull, you've cooked it too long.

When the mushrooms and tofu are finished cooking, toss them together in enough of the warm sauce to coat evenly. Transfer the broccoli and the mushroom and tofu mixture to individual serving plates or a serving platter, top with the green onions and Sriracha (if using), and serve with the rice.

CAROLYN'S MICROWAVE SHORTCUT: I may or may not have learned this technique from my mom in the 1980s. Place the Chinese broccoli in a microwave-safe bowl with 2 tablespoons water. Cover it with plastic wrap and microwave for 1½ minutes. Remove from the microwave and allow the broccoli to steam for a few minutes under the plastic. Drain before using. And don't judge me.

Rice bran oil for deep-frying (optional)

3 cups cut or torn oyster mushrooms, in 1-inch pieces

1 package (10 oz) Hodo organic firm tofu, cut into 1-inch pieces

1 bunch Chinese broccoli or water spinach (ong choy), cut into 1-inch pieces

4 tablespoons finely sliced green onions

1 tablespoon Sriracha sauce or sambal oelek for serving (optional)

2 cups cooked brown rice, hot

NOTE: If you don't have a thermometer, you can gauge the temperature by standing the handle of a wooden spoon (or a wooden chopstick) in the hot oil. If bubbles gather around the handle and float up to the surface, you've got the correct temperature. If the oil is visibly bubbling, it's too hot.

FANCY-TASTING IMPOSSIBLE BURGER

I know, I know, it's a burger. Do we really need a recipe for a burger? Well, there are a few simple things you can do to take plant-based ground beef to the next level. Here, we offer steps to make what we consider to be the platonic ideal of an Impossible burger. The iceberg lettuce and sauce add fast-food nostalgia. But little things—the brioche bun, the liquid smoke, the pickled pan-seared onion slices—take it up a notch. We like Impossible meat the best. However, we've tried Beyond, Pure Farmland, and Lightlife products, which will all work well in a pinch.

 THE PLAN: Make the sauce and onions and ready the fixings. Then season and cook the burgers, toast the buns, and assemble the burgers.

To make the sauce, in a small bowl, combine all the ingredients and mix well. Set aside.

To prepare the onion, slice the onion horizontally ¼–½ inch thick, keeping the rings intact. Season the slices with salt and pepper and drizzle with the olive oil. In a small bowl, stir together the vinegar, water, sugar, and ½ teaspoon salt until the sugar and salt dissolve. Heat a heavy-bottomed sauté pan over medium-high heat. When the pan is hot, add the onion slices in a single layer and sear until the underside is evenly caramelized, about 2 minutes. Immediately transfer the slices to a small airtight container, pour in the vinegar mixture, and cap tightly. The carryover heat will continue to cook the onions while they are pickling in the liquid.

If you are using premade patties, season each patty with salt and pepper and 6 drops of the liquid smoke. If you are using ground burger meat, add the liquid smoke to it, mix well, divide in half, and shape into patties. Season the patties with salt and pepper.

To cook the burgers, heat a frying pan over medium-high heat until very hot but not smoking. Add the rice bran oil and then the patties to the pan. Sear, turning once, until a deep brown crust forms on both sides, about 2 minutes on each side. The idea is to develop the crust without overcooking and drying out the center. If you like a medium-rare burger, pull the burger off the heat as soon as both sides are seared. If you prefer a more well-done burger, cook for a few more minutes over medium heat.

To assemble the burgers, place the bun bottoms, cut side up, on individual plates. Lay a nice layer of sauce on each bun bottom (and the bun top, if you like). Pull the onion slices from their pickling liquid and arrange them on the sauce. Add the burgers, then top with the cheese, tomato, and lettuce. Close with the bun tops and serve.

NOTE: Ideally, you will have a ripe tomato for these burgers, but if you can't find one, oven-roasted plum tomatoes are an acceptable stand-in. Preheat the oven to 400°F. Line a sheet pan with aluminum foil. Cut the tomatoes in half, drizzle them with extra-virgin olive oil, and season with salt and pepper. Place the tomatoes, cut side up, on the prepared pan and roast until the skins start to burst, about 40 minutes.

FOR THE SAUCE

½ cup Just Mayo

3 tablespoons ketchup

2 tablespoons Sriracha sauce

1 tablespoon pickle juice (from a jar of pickles)

¼ teaspoon onion powder

FOR THE PICKLED ONION

1 red onion

Kosher salt and freshly ground black pepper

2 tablespoons extra-virgin olive or rice bran oil

½ cup balsamic, red wine, or sherry vinegar

½ cup water

1 tablespoon organic sugar

Two ¼-lb plant-based burger patties, or ½ lb ground plant-based burger meat

Kosher salt and freshly ground black pepper

12 drops liquid smoke

2 tablespoons rice bran oil

2 brioche buns, split and toasted

2 slices plant-based Cheddar or other cheese, preferably Violife brand

4–6 thin ripe tomato slices (see Note)

1 cup shredded iceberg or butter lettuce

Sides

CURRIED CAULIFLOWER WITH MUHAMMARA

What is it with cauliflower these days? Everyone loves it! The punch of bold flavors in this dish makes it a real crowd-pleaser. We think roasting the cauliflower brings out the best taste and texture, but you can sauté or fry it if you prefer.

If you cannot find pomegranate seeds, raw or roasted grapes will work nicely as a substitute. You can also use pine nuts or almonds instead of walnuts. Curry powder comes in a dramatic array of variations. The nicer ones are a bit more expensive, but they are well worth it.

THE PLAN: Turn on the oven to 300°F and toast the walnuts for both the muhammara (if you don't already have it on hand) and the cauliflower as it heats, then crank up the oven to 450°F for cooking the cauliflower. Next, get the cauliflower cut and roasting, then work on the remaining ingredients. Everything comes together in a big bowl just before serving.

Position an oven rack in the upper third of the oven and preheat the oven to 450°F. Line a sheet pan with aluminum foil.

Cut the cauliflower into roughly 1½-inch pieces. The pieces will shrink about 30 percent during roasting, so you don't want to cut them too small. Also, the center and ribs as well as the florets can be cooked and eaten. Put the pieces into a large bowl, add the oil, and toss to coat evenly. Then season the oiled cauliflower with the curry powder and generously with salt, mixing well.

Spread the cauliflower on the prepared pan. Roast the cauliflower on the top rack of the oven until light brown, about 30 minutes. (The top rack is important here because many home ovens heat from the bottom, and the cauliflower can burn if positioned lower.) Remove from the oven.

Pick the cilantro sprigs into 3-inch lengths. (The stems are the best part, so we don't want to exclude them.) Spoon the muhammara into the center of a serving bowl or plate. Using a circular motion, spread it as if spreading tomato sauce on a pizza crust, leaving a couple of inches of the bowl or plate rim uncovered. In a large bowl, toss the cauliflower with the cilantro, pomegranate seeds, and walnuts. Spoon the cauliflower mixture into the center of the muhammara pool. Garnish the top of the dish with any stragglers in the bowl and serve.

1 head cauliflower, any color

¼ cup olive oil

2 tablespoons Madras or Japanese curry powder

Kosher salt

½ bunch fresh cilantro

¼ cup Muhammara (page 162)

¼ cup pomegranate seeds

½ cup walnut halves, toasted and broken in half (see Note, page 33)

SHISHITO PEPPERS WITH PRESERVED LEMON & CELERY

Shishito peppers are found in the appetizer section of many restaurant menus these days. While they may seem cheffy, they are easy to prepare at home. Hearts of celery, the inner yellow ribs lurking within every celery head, add another layer of flavor. More tender and less bitter than the outer, more fibrous green ribs, they are a secret super ingredient hidden in plain sight.

When cooking the peppers, keep in mind that undercooking is preferred to overcooking. These guys have very thin walls, and the internal steam helps continue the cooking after you remove them from the heat. Even if the charred color is not quite there yet, pull them off and test one with a little salt to see how it tastes.

THE PLAN: If grilling, start the grill. Pick the leaves from the celery heart and thinly slice the ribs. Cook the peppers, toss with the celery slices, olives, and seasoning, top with the celery leaves and serve.

Remove the outer green ribs of the celery head until you reach the yellow center. Save the green parts for another use. Pull away 1 or 2 of the yellow branches, choosing the ones with the most leaves. Pick the leaves and save them to use as a garnish. Using a mandoline or a sharp knife, slice the ribs as thinly as possible until you have ½ cup slices. Set aside.

You can cook the peppers on a grill or on the stove top. To grill the peppers, prepare the grill for direct cooking over high heat. Thread the peppers onto sets of paired skewers held about 1 inch apart, piercing the tip and the stem end of each pepper. (Paired skewers make the peppers easier to flip on the grill.) Place the peppers directly over the fire and grill, turning once, until charred on both sides, about 1½ minutes on each side.

To cook the peppers on the stove top, line a plate with paper towels and set it near the stove. Place a large sauté pan over high heat and wait for about 2 minutes. Meanwhile, open a window or two because this method is going to create smoke. The pan is ready when a few drops of oil smoke immediately on contact. Add the oil and count to 10. Then add the peppers. If you have done everything correctly, they will pop, so be careful and keep a little distance. Cook for about 1 minute. Then, using a long spoon or tongs, turn the peppers over and cook for another minute. Blair usually cooks them only on two sides so that they don't overcook.

When the peppers are done to your liking—at our house, this usually takes 3-4 minutes total—pull the pan off the heat and transfer the peppers to the towel-lined plate to drain.

Put the peppers and olives into a metal bowl and sprinkle them with the celery slices as if sprinkling cheese on a pizza. Then sprinkle the lemon zest and the salt to taste on top and toss to mix evenly.

Place a paper towel in the bottom of a serving bowl and spoon in the pepper mixture. Top with the reserved celery leaves and serve.

1 head celery

1 lb shishito or Padrón peppers

½ cup Castelvetrano olives

Olive oil, if cooking on the stove top

Grated zest of ½ lemon

Maldon sea salt

BROCCOLINI WITH
MISO BAGNA CAUDA

Bagna cauda functions a lot like fondue: just substitute bubbling garlic-steeped olive oil for the cheese. Decades ago in northern Italy, Blair attended a bagna cauda dinner that has since reached mythical proportions. A room full of communal tables greeted him with a blast of garlic-drenched air, so the story goes. He went on to feast for hours on vegetables and breads dipped in the pungent oil. Garlic wafted from his pores for days. (Thankfully, I had not yet met Blair.)

Now, if you have an Italian grandmother, please do not allow her to read beyond this point. The problem with bagna cauda for plant-based eaters is that it contains anchovies. This recipe calls for umami-rich miso and tahini which make up for the bold flavor traditionally provided by anchovies.

 THE PLAN: First, roast the garlic. Prepare the garnishes. Next, if grilling the broccolini, start the grill. Then make the sauce, cook the broccolini, and serve.

To make the sauce, preheat the oven to 375°F. While the oven is heating, lay a sheet of aluminum foil on a work surface. Peel all the garlic cloves, putting them on the foil as you work. When all the garlic is peeled, drizzle the cloves with 1 tablespoon of the oil and toss to coat evenly. Bring up the opposite edges of the foil and fold them together a few times to ensure a tight seal. Then fold up each end and seal tightly to create a secure packet.

Place the packet in the oven and roast the garlic until golden and soft, 40-50 minutes. Remove the packet from the oven, open it, and pour the contents into a bowl. Add the remaining 3 tablespoons oil, the miso, tahini, lemon juice, Aleppo pepper, and salt and stir to mix well. Set aside.

You can cook the broccolini on a grill or on the stove top. To cook the broccolini on a grill, prepare the grill for direct cooking over medium-high heat. In a bowl, toss the broccolini with the oil and a pinch of salt, coating evenly. Place the broccolini perpendicular to the bars of the grill rack directly over the fire and grill until you see some dark color on the underside, 1-2 minutes. Flip the broccolini over and grill on the second side until browned, 1-2 minutes. Transfer to a cutting board, let cool for a few minutes, and then cut into 2-inch lengths.

To cook the broccolini on the stove top, cut it into 2-inch lengths and season with salt. In a large sauté pan, heat the oil over medium-high heat. Add the broccolini in a single layer and cook undisturbed until the underside is a nice dark brown, about 5 minutes. Remove from the heat. (Cooking on one side only until caramelized creates a nice depth of flavor.)

To plate, lightly drizzle the sauce across the bottom of each individual serving plate. Place a mound of the broccolini in the center of each plate, dividing it evenly. Drain the radishes and fennel and pat them dry. Garnish the broccoli with the radishes, fennel, and parsley stems and serve.

FOR THE SAUCE

2 heads garlic

4 tablespoons pungent extra-virgin olive oil

2 tablespoons white (shiro) miso

2 tablespoons Joyva tahini

1 tablespoon fresh lemon juice

½ teaspoon Aleppo pepper

½ teaspoon kosher salt

1 lb broccolini

1 tablespoon extra-virgin olive oil

Kosher salt

2 red radishes, sliced paper-thin and soaked in cold water

1 fennel bulb, sliced crosswise paper-thin and soaked in cold water

½ teaspoon minced fresh flat-leaf parsley stems

SMASHED CUCUMBERS WITH SESAME, CILANTRO & VINEGAR

Smashed, garlicky cucumber salad sets off spicier dishes with its vinegary, somewhat sweet dressing. Chefs love to play with this dish, making it spicier, sweeter, or more acidic to fit their tastes. We think our version is fairly balanced and satisfying, even without the heat. Sometimes we make this dish into a light meal by adding green beans and avocado. And don't pigeonhole this recipe into an Asian menu. This dish goes well with just about any cuisine.

 THE PLAN: Smash the cucumber, salt it, and let it sit for 10 minutes, then drain and toss with the remaining ingredients.

Place the cucumber on a cutting boeard and, using the back of a large chef's knife or a rolling pin, gently "smash" it. You're not trying to flatten it. You simply want to crack it open so the outside tears. Cut the smashed cucumber into 1-inch-long pieces. Transfer the pieces to a bowl, season with the salt, and let sit for 10 minutes. (This step is the key to big flavor!)

Drain off any liquid from the bowl. Add the vinegar, oil, cilantro, garlic, sugar, and sesame seeds, toss lightly to mix evenly, and serve.

NOTE: If you cannot find an English or Japanese cucumber, choose any cucumber with a thin skin or peel a common slicing cucumber. If you cannot find seasoned rice vinegar, dissolve ¼ teaspoon organic sugar and a pinch of kosher salt in 1 tablespoon regular rice vinegar.

½ lb Japanese or English cucumber (see Note)

½ teaspoon kosher salt

1 tablespoon seasoned rice vinegar (see Note)

½ teaspoon toasted sesame oil

1 tablespoon chopped fresh cilantro

2 teaspoons minced garlic

1 teaspoon organic sugar

½ teaspoon sesame seeds

ROASTED MARBLE POTATOES WITH BLACK GARLIC & CHARRED GREEN ONION AIOLI

If you like bold and bright flavors, this one will really blow your hair back. Take that, potato salad! A few years back, black garlic hit peak trend among professional chefs. This had the nice side effect of making it more readily available in supermarkets for home cooks.

So what exactly *is* black garlic? It's basically garlic that is heated at a very low temperature over a long period, such as two to three weeks, to develop a flavor that's akin to the richness of Worcestershire but sweeter and without any bite. Fun to experiment with, it is sold in jars in fancy grocery stores, some Asian markets, and online. If you cannot find it, Worcestershire sauce can be substituted.

Now about these potatoes. The smashing method we illustrate here allows the roasting oil to penetrate into their cracks and crevices, creating magical crunchy bits around the edges. They are truly the best part of this dish. We can't wait for you to see for yourself.

 THE PLAN: Cook the potatoes in water, then give them a gentle smash before roasting until crispy. While the potatoes are roasting, get everything else ready.

Preheat the oven to 450°F. Line a roasting pan large enough to hold the potatoes in a single layer with aluminum foil.

While the oven is preheating, bring a large pot of water to a boil over high heat. Add the potatoes, reduce the heat to medium, and cook until tender when pierced with the tip of a knife, about 10 minutes.

Drain the potatoes and allow the steam to dissipate for 1 minute. (This ensures the water fully evaporates, preventing the potatoes from sticking in the roasting pan.) Put the warm potatoes on a cutting board, grab a dinner plate or other hard, flat kitchen object, place it on top of 5-8 potatoes, and press down gently but firmly, smashing them by about 30 percent so the skin cracks. (You do not want to turn them into pancakes.) Repeat until all the potatoes are smashed.

Transfer the potatoes to the prepared pan and spread in a single layer. Drizzle with the oil, sprinkle with the salt, and toss to coat evenly. Roast the potatoes, stirring them twice at 15-minute intervals, until they are crisp on the outside and starting to brown, about 45 minutes.

While the potatoes roast, make the black garlic sauce. If using black garlic, peel the cloves if they are not peeled, then put a clove on a cutting board. Using the flat side of a large chef's knife, smash the clove, then scrape the knife toward you while continuing to press down on the garlic. Repeat the scraping several times until the clove is reduced

FOR THE POTATOES

2 ½ lb mixed marble or baby potatoes

2 tablespoons extra-virgin olive oil

½ teaspoon kosher salt

⅓ cup black garlic sauce (below)

⅓ cup thinly sliced red radishes (2-3 radishes, preferably sliced on a mandoline)

Leaves from ¼ bunch fresh dill

FOR THE BLACK GARLIC SAUCE

About ¼ cup black garlic cloves, or 2 tablespoons plant-based Worcestershire sauce

1 tablespoon rice vinegar

½ teaspoon kosher salt

½ teaspoon raw cane sugar

3 tablespoons extra-virgin olive oil

FOR THE AIOLI

½ teaspoon extra-virgin olive oil

½ bunch green onions, roots trimmed and dry outer layer removed

½ cup Just Mayo

½ teaspoon kosher salt

¼ teaspoon freshly ground black pepper

Grated zest of 1 lemon

Squeeze of fresh lemon juice for finishing

to a fine paste. Repeat with the remaining cloves until you have ¼ cup paste. Scoop the garlic paste into a small bowl. If using Worcestershire sauce, pour it into a small bowl. Add the vinegar, salt, and sugar to the bowl and mix well, then add the oil and whisk until incorporated. It's okay if it's not perfectly emulsified. You should have about ⅓ cup sauce. Set the sauce aside for tossing with the potatoes.

To make the aioli, first char the green onions. In a sauté pan, heat the oil over high heat until it begins to smoke. (Make sure your hood fan is on, or open a couple of windows to get a cross breeze going in your kitchen!) Add the onions in a single layer and keep them in one place until they get a nice dark char on the underside, 1-2 minutes on high heat. If you really enjoy charred flavor, go ahead and char them on the other side as well. Remove from the heat and let cool slightly.

Transfer the charred onions to a food processor and pulse until a chunky paste forms. Or transfer them to a cutting board and mince by hand.

Put the mayonnaise into a small bowl and fold in the onions until evenly distributed. Season with the salt, pepper, and lemon zest. Set aside.

When the potatoes are ready, remove from the oven and let cool in the pan for 3–5 minutes. Transfer the potatoes to a large bowl, add the black garlic sauce and most of the radish slices and dill (reserve some of both for garnish), and toss to mix evenly.

Transfer the potatoes to a serving bowl and garnish with the reserved dill and radish slices and the squeeze of lemon juice. Serve with the aioli on the side for dipping.

BRUSSELS SPROUTS WITH CHILE, LIME, CRISPY ONIONS & COOLING HERBS

In the 1990s, a Dutch scientist changed brussels sprouts forever by figuring out which compound made them bitter and then working to extract it. Chef David Chang was one of the first chefs to latch on to this new version. In 2006, he opened the now-iconic Momofuku Ssäm Bar in Manhattan, serving a dish similar to this one, which kicked off a veritable Brussels sprouts renaissance in America.

Fast-forward to today, and restaurants all over the world serve brussels sprouts like these, and they can't take them off the menu. The layered salt, sweet, and sour flavors, along with different textures, make for a completely addictive, mind-bending bite each time. But because the dish includes fish sauce, plant-based eaters have never been able to enjoy it—until now. If you have time, make Blair's homemade no-fish sauce. If not, use store-bought Tofuna or another brand, though it will create a slightly different flavor profile.

THE PLAN: If making the fish sauce from scratch, you'll need to start 24 hours in advance. Cut and roast the brussels sprouts, then prep the sauce and herbs while the sprouts roast.

Preheat the oven to 400°F.

To trim and cut the brussels sprouts, nip the end of each stem if it is bruised or dark, then remove the outermost layer of leaves. Cut the sprouts lengthwise into halves or quarters, depending on the size of the sprouts. You want a couple of pieces to fit on a spoon per bite. In a large bowl, toss the sprouts with the oil, coating them evenly.

Spread the sprouts in a single layer on a sheet pan (reserve the bowl). Roast the sprouts, stirring them and rotating the pan back to front after 15 minutes, until crispy, about 35 minutes.

While the sprouts roast, make the sauce. In a small bowl, whisk together the lime juice, fish sauce, water, sugar, and Sriracha (if using) until the sugar dissolves. Set aside.

Tear the larger mint leaves into bite-size pieces. Pick cilantro leaves with stems intact into 2-inch-long pieces, or if using basil, tear larger leaves into bite-size pieces.

When the sprouts are ready, return them to the reserved bowl. Add the sauce and herbs and toss well. The sprouts will be swimming in the sauce a bit, but that's what you want. Spoon or ladle the mixture into a serving bowl or individual bowls, garnish with the onions, and serve.

½ lb brussels sprouts

¼ cup olive oil

¼ cup fresh lime juice

2 tablespoons No-Fish Sauce (page 161)

2 tablespoons water

3 tablespoons raw cane, date, or coconut sugar

1 teaspoon Sriracha sauce (optional)

¼ cup loosely packed stemmed fresh mint leaves

¼ cup loosely packed fresh cilantro with stems or basil leaves

2 tablespoons fried onions, preferably French's brand

WEEKNIGHT CORN BREAD

Blair ate a lot of corn bread as a kid growing up in Atlanta in the 1980s. (Little did he know that his future wife was subsisting on Poppin' Fresh Pillsbury crescent rolls outside Philadelphia.) Even though it was an every day affair for Blair, weeknight corn bread makes me feel fancy to this day. This vegan version comes together in about a half hour. Eat it with the Truffle Butter on page 160, the Barbecue Spread on page 103, or straight out of the container of leftovers like a heathen.

 THE PLAN: You guys, it's so easy—just mix it and bake it!

Preheat the oven to 400°F. Lightly grease an 8-inch square or 9-inch round cake pan.

In a large bowl, stir together the flour, cornmeal, sugar, baking powder, and salt. In Pour the soy milk and canola oil into another bowl and stir until well mixed. Melt the butter for 30 seconds in the microwave and add to the milk mixture along with the lemon juice and corn kernels, stirring to mix. Using a spatula, carefully fold the wet mixture into the dry ingredients stirring until combined. Pour the batter into the prepared pan.

Bake the corn bread until the top is browned and a toothpick inserted into the center comes out clean, 25–30 minutes. Let cool in the pan on a wire rack for 10 minutes before cutting and serving.

NOTE: If you want real southerner credibility, you need to bake this bread in a round cast-iron pan. That said, you are using soy milk and vegan butter, so you should probably just forget about southern credibility and bake this corn bread however the heck you want.

⅓ cup Miyoko's unsalted butter, plus more for the pan and eating

1¼ cups all-purpose flour

1 cup yellow cornmeal

½ cup sugar

1 tablespoon baking powder

1 teaspoon kosher salt

1¼ cups soy milk

1 tablespoon fresh lemon juice or cider vinegar

1 tablespoon Bob's Red Mill Egg Replacer, prepared for 1 whole egg according to package directions

1 cup fresh or frozen corn kernels

SKIN-ON FRIES

If you are a fan of fries that have craggy, crispy bits, this is the recipe for you. Making sure the oil is always at the correct temperature is key to success, so a deep-frying thermometer is handy to have. If you lack a thermometer, see the Note on page 70 for an easy workaround.

THE PLAN: Cut the potatoes, cook them partially in water, then dry, let them cool completely, and deep-fry.

Fill a large bowl with water and add the vinegar. You will be soaking the potatoes in this acidulated water, which helps keep them nice and white. Wash each potato, then square off the sides and end with a sharp knife. Now slide the knife through the potato to cut it into slabs between ¼ and ½ inch thick. Line up the slabs and cut them into ¼-inch-thick fries, dropping the fries into the acidulated water as you go.

Once all the fries are in the bowl, rinse them in the bowl under cold running water until the water runs clear from the bowl. The idea is to rinse off any excess starch, which would prematurely brown in frying.

Fill a large pot with salted water and bring to a boil over high heat. Lay a clean kitchen towel on a work surface near the stove. Add the fries to the boiling water, adjust the heat to a gentle simmer, and simmer the fries just until they are about to start crumbling, 8–10 minutes. This step creates all the little crags and cracks that get nice and crunchy when you fry the potatoes. Watch closely, as a minute or two too long and you have potato soup.

Using a wire skimmer or a fish spatula, ever so gently transfer the potatoes to the towel and pat them dry. For best results, let them cool completely before frying, which can take up to 1 hour. Discard the water, wipe the pot dry, and reserve.

Line a large plate with paper towels and set it near the stove. Pour the oil to a depth of about 3 inches into the reserved pot and heat to 375°F on a deep-frying thermometer. Working in batches to avoid crowding, add the potatoes to the hot oil and fry, turning frequently, until golden brown, 3–4 minutes. Using the wire skimmer or fish spatula, transfer them to the towel-lined plate to drain. Repeat until all the potatoes are fried.

Season the hot fries generously with salt and serve.

2 tablespoons distilled white, malt, or cider vinegar

2 or 3 large russet potatoes

Rice bran oil for deep-frying

Kosher salt

HARISSA GRILLED CARROTS
WITH LEMON CREMA

When you think of cooking carrots, grilling is probably not the first thing that comes to mind. But trust us here: just about anything tastes better cooked on a wood-fired grill. That said, roasting in the oven is a solid second choice (see Note). This dish strikes the balance of sweet, salty, spicy, and cool. It also provides a pop of bold color on any table. It's the sleeper hit of many a meal.

THE PLAN: If you peel baby carrots, you are left with very little, so we use them with their skin on here. Prep and marinate the carrots. You can prep the lemon crema and mint and start the grill while the carrots are marinating. Then cook the carrots, dress, garnish, and serve.

Immerse the carrots in a large bowl or sinkful of cold water and leave to soak for about 20 minutes to free up any dirt and grit. Scrub off any persistent dirt with a towel or a clean green scour pad (the type you use to wash pots). If you use a scour pad, you'll take off the first super-thin layer of carrot skin, which makes the carrot color a bit more vibrant! Dry the carrots well, then transfer to a bowl, add the harissa, about 1 teaspoon salt, and 2 tablespoons of the oil, and toss well. Let marinate for at least 20 minutes. If you can plan ahead and marinate them for a few hours, they'll taste even better.

While the carrots are marinating, make the lemon crema. In a small bowl, combine the sour cream, the remaining 2 tablespoons oil, the lemon zest and juice, and about 1 teaspoon salt and mix well. Pick the most beautiful mint leaves from the sprigs and reserve the leaves for garnish.

Prepare the grill for indirect cooking over medium-low heat. Arrange the carrots perpendicular to the bars of the grill rack over indirect heat and grill for about 10 minutes. They are ready when they have browned a little and are just tender when pierced with a knife tip.

Transfer the carrots to a serving platter. To dress them with the crema, scoop up a spoonful of the crema and, holding the spoon like a pen, move it back and forth over the carrots in a zigzag motion. Sprinkle the mint leaves on top and, if you want a little extra drama, dust a bit of harissa on the plate as well, then serve.

NOTE: If only larger carrots are available, cut them into sticks the width of a middle finger and blanch them for 2 minutes before grilling them. You can roast the carrots in the oven rather than grill them. Preheat the oven to 400°F. Spread the carrots in a single layer on a sheet pan and roast, turning once and rotating the pan back to front after 15 minutes, until browned and just tender when pierced with a knife tip, about 30 minutes.

1 bunch baby rainbow carrots (see Note)

2 tablespoons harissa seasoning (dry spice blend), plus more for garnish (optional)

Kosher salt

4 tablespoons olive oil

½ cup Tofutti sour cream

Grated zest of 1 lemon

Juice of ½ lemon

2–3 fresh mint sprigs

JAPANESE POTATOES
WITH ROASTED NORI BUTTER

These purple beauties are loaded with essential vitamins, minerals, and antioxidants and are said to help lower blood pressure and blood-sugar levels. Here, we punch up the flavor with plant-based butter and nori-laced furikake, a common Japanese table condiment. It's amazing how these simple ingredients come together to create something that's healthy but addictively delicious. If you cannot find baby potatoes, buy larger ones and cut them into 3-inch chunks.

 THE PLAN: Make the butter while the potatoes are baking, then combine and serve.

Position an oven rack in the upper third of the oven and preheat the oven to 450°F. Remove the butter from the refrigerator and bring it to room temperature.

Lay a large sheet of aluminum foil on a work surface and place the potatoes on the foil. Season the potatoes evenly with the kosher salt and drizzle evenly with the oil, adding more salt and oil if needed to coat evenly. Then bring up the opposite edges of the foil and fold them together a few times to ensure a tight seal. Then fold up each end and seal tightly to create a secure packet.

Place the foil packet on the top rack of the oven and bake the potatoes until fork-tender, about 20 minutes.

While the potatoes are baking, in a small bowl, work together the butter and furikake with a metal spoon or fork until evenly mixed. Cover and refrigerate to allow the flavors to come together.

When the potatoes are ready, unwrap them and let them cool for a bit. Then crack them open by either applying firm pressure to the outside or cutting with a knife. Place an equal amount of the butter into the crack of each potato, sprinkle lightly with sea salt, and serve.

4 tablespoons Myoko's unsalted butter

2 lb baby purple potatoes

2 tablespoons kosher salt, or as needed

3 tablespoons olive oil, or as needed

2 tablespoons nori komi furikake or other furikake of choice

Maldon sea salt for sprinkling

WOK-FIRED ASPARAGUS WITH LEMON, GINGER & TAHINI

This recipe is one of those happy accidents. One night when we were out of sesame seeds, Blair tossed tahini into the wok with asparagus and the result was miraculous. The tahini lightly blanketed the asparagus in the flavor of toasted sesame and—the best part—our son, James, ate asparagus for the very first time. The key to this dish is to allow the asparagus to sit in the wok without stirring it for seconds at a time so the exterior sears. We eat this at least once a week during asparagus season.

 THE PLAN: Prep all the ingredients, then cook the aromatics and asparagus, add the tahini, and serve.

Place a wok or large sauté pan over high heat and wait for 2 minutes until it is very hot. Add the oil and wait for 5 seconds. Add the ginger and garlic while stirring for 5 seconds. Add the asparagus, stir once, then allow the asparagus to sit undisturbed for 10 seconds as it sears and steams. Stir and then repeat the sitting followed by the stirring three to five times until the asparagus is evenly seared and cooked tender yet firm to the bite.

Add the tahini and salt to the pan and immediately pull the pan off the heat while stirring vigorously. Transfer the asparagus to a serving bowl, drizzle with the lemon juice and toss to coat evenly. Garnish with the lemon zest and sesame seeds (if using) and serve.

2 tablespoons canola or rice bran oil

2 teaspoons peeled and finely minced fresh ginger (mince to a paste)

2 teaspoons finely minced garlic (mince to a paste)

1 bunch asparagus, woody ends removed and spears cut on the diagonal into 1½-inch lengths

2 tablespoons Joyva tahini

½ teaspoon kosher salt

Grated zest and juice of 1 lemon

½ teaspoon toasted sesame seeds (optional)

TRUFFLE BUTTER MASHED POTATOES

This potato dish is loosely based on legendary chef Joël Robuchon's famous potato purée recipe—often referred to as the best mashed potatoes in the world. Although Robuchon died in 2018, his potato recipe lives on at his restaurants in Europe, Asia, and North America and is taught in culinary schools across the world. The Robuchon version calls for a two-to-one ratio of potato to butter. Although we don't quite go to that extreme here, rest assured our dish will be rich and delicious all the same.

THE PLAN: Begin cooking the potatoes. Meanwhile, make the cashew cream. Then process the potatoes and mix the ingredients together.

Put the potatoes into a large pot of salted water and bring to a boil over high heat. Cook the potatoes until very tender, about 30 minutes. Drain, let cool until they can be handled, then peel and set aside in a large bowl. Reserve the pot.

While the potatoes are cooking, in a blender, combine the cashews and water and blend until very smooth and cream-like. Set aside.

Pass the potatoes through a food mill or potato ricer (not a food processor) back into the pot. Place the pot over medium heat and heat, stirring, until the excess moisture evaporates, about 1 minute. Remove from the heat, add the cashew cream and truffle butter, and stir until incorporated. Season to taste with salt.

Transfer to a serving bowl, garnish with chives, if using, and serve.

2½ lb Yukon gold potatoes

Kosher salt

½ cup cashews

1 cup water or soy milk

4 tablespoons Truffle Butter (page 160)

Minced fresh chives for garnish (optional)

Snacks
& Crowd-
Pleasers

GREEN PEA FALAFEL WITH MINT-GARLIC WHITE SAUCE

This version of falafel consists mostly of peas and quinoa, making for a very fluffy texture that crisps up just the way you want it to. The green of the interior is quite striking, so if you are considering these for a dinner party, do it. The recipe is also easy enough to make for a regular weeknight dinner at home, and you'll probably have some leftovers.

 THE PLAN: Prep all the ingredients and make the falafel batter. Scoop and bake or fry.

In a food processor, combine the spinach, parsley, mint, garlic, coriander, cumin, paprika, turmeric, and ½ teaspoon salt and pulse until all the ingredients are well incorporated and the garlic is broken into small pieces. Add the peas and process until smooth.

In a large bowl, stir together the quinoa, egg replacer, and flour. Add the pea mixture and stir until well mixed. Using a tablespoon measure, scoop up the quinoa-pea mixture and shape into 2-tablespoon-size balls, setting them aside on a sheet pan as they are formed. You should have about 20 balls.

The falafel can be deep-fried or baked. To deep-fry the falafel, line a large plate with paper towels and set it near the stove. Pour the rice bran oil to a depth of 2 inches into a deep, heavy pot and heat to 375°F on a deep-frying thermometer (see Note, page 70). Working in batches to avoid crowding, carefully drop the balls into the hot oil and fry until crispy on the outside and soft and bright green on the inside, about 5 minutes. Using a wire skimmer, transfer to the towel-lined plate to drain and season with a pinch of salt. Repeat until all the balls or cooked.

To bake the falafel, preheat the oven to 350°F. Line a sheet pan with parchment paper. Brush the bottom of each falafel ball with olive oil and place, bottom side down, on the prepared sheet pan, spacing them well apart. Bake the balls until crispy on the outside and soft and green on the inside, about 30 minutes.

To plate the falafel, spread a little white sauce on each individual serving plate, top with the falafel, sprinkle with pickled onions, and serve the flatbread on the side.

1 ½ cups tightly packed spinach, large stems removed

1 tablespoon fresh flat-leaf parsley leaves

1 tablespoon stemmed fresh mint leaves

1 medium clove garlic

1 teaspoon ground coriander

1 teaspoon ground cumin

1 teaspoon smoked paprika

1 teaspoon ground turmeric

Kosher salt

2 ½ cups frozen English peas

1 ½ cups cooked quinoa

1 tablespoon Bob's Red Mill Egg Replacer, prepared for 1 whole egg according to package directions

¼ cup buckwheat flour

Rice bran oil or vegetable oil if deep-frying

Extra-virgin olive oil for brushing if baking

Mint-Garlic White Sauce, homemade (page 155) or store-bought

Pickled onions, homemade (page 154) or store-bought

Lavash or other flatbread for serving

SPROUTED & SMOKED NUTS

If you are not yet a sprouter of nuts, please pull up a chair and settle in for a minute so we can convert you. Sprouting nuts (and seeds!) makes it easier for your body to absorb their inherent nutrients and also makes them easier to digest. A cute little stem also springs out of the nut, which is fun to see!

For this sprouted and smoked nut recipe, we use liquid smoke to flavor the mix. This serves two purposes. It saves you the time it would take to smoke nuts yourself, but, more important, it allows you to keep the heat level low while you are toasting the nuts, which preserves more of their nutrients.

 THE PLAN: Soak and sprout the nuts for 24 hours. Toast the nuts for 12 hours, then toss with the seasonings.

In a container with a cover, combine all the nuts, 2 tablespoons of the salt, the liquid smoke, and the 2 cups water, adding more water if needed to immerse fully. Cover the container and let sit at room temperature for 24 hours.

Drain the nuts well, discarding the water. Preheat the oven to 150°F. Spread the nuts in a single layer on a sheet pan and toast until crunchy, about 12 hours.

Pour the warm nuts into a large bowl. Add the rosemary, thyme, sugar, orange zest, the remaining 1 teaspoon salt, and the oil and stir and toss to coat the nuts evenly with the seasonings. Transfer to a serving bowl and serve. Leftover nuts will keep in an airtight container at room temperature for up to 2 weeks.

1 cup raw almonds

1 cup raw cashews

1 cup raw pecans

1 cup raw walnuts

2 tablespoons plus 1 teaspoon kosher salt

1 tablespoon liquid smoke

2 cups water, or as needed

2 tablespoons fresh rosemary leaves

2 tablespoons fresh thyme leaves

1 teaspoon raw cane sugar

Grated zest of 1 orange

1 tablespoon olive oil

KING TRUMPET MUSHROOM CEVICHE

Leche de tigre, "tiger's milk" in Spanish, is the liquid that's left over when you cure fish in citrus and spice to make ceviche. It's said to have aphrodisiac effects and is so prized that restaurants frequently serve it in a small glass alongside the ceviche. Yes, you can drink it straight. The flavor is that outstanding.

We use a classic curing mixture to make this plant-based ceviche. The steamed, sliced mushroom stems resemble scallops. Their mild flavor is a good foil for the bold flavors of the other ingredients, and their texture holds up beautifully to the chunky mix of tomato, onion, cucumber, and avocado. When you're deciding which chips to use, follow your whimsy. We buy either taqueria-style bold blue corn or "healthier" chips with flaxseeds, depending on our mood. Whatever you choose, this dish is an astoundingly close replica to the fish seafood version that inspired it.

 THE PLAN: Soak the radish slices. Make the leche de tigre. Then steam the mushrooms, chop the vegetables and mango, and toss everything together to serve.

To make the leche de tigre, in a blender, combine all the ingredients and blend until well combined. Let sit for 5 minutes, then strain through a fine-mesh sieve into a bowl. Measure out 1 cup leche de tigre for the ceviche. The leftover liquid will keep in an airtight container in the refrigerator for up to 1 week.

Steam the mushrooms for 2 minutes, then let cool. In a bowl, combine the steamed mushrooms, cherry tomatoes, cucumber, radish, onion, cilantro stems, and the 1 cup leche de tigre and mix gently. Season to taste with salt. It's best to let this mixture sit for 10–15 minutes so the flavors come together. But if you can't wait, toss in the mango and avocado now. The ceviche will still be quite delicious. Adding the avocado and mango at the end keeps the flavors cleaner.

Spoon the ceviche mixture into a bowl and garnish with the cilantro sprigs. Serve the tortilla chips on the side.

FOR THE LECHE DE TIGRE

½ cup canned diced fire-roasted tomatoes

¼ cup fresh lime juice

½ cup water ice-cold water

1 ½ tablespoons roughly chopped red onion

1 tablespoon finely chopped fresh cilantro stems

½ clove garlic

½ teaspoon grated unpeeled fresh ginger

½ teaspoon aji amarillo or rocoto pepper paste, or ¼ habanero chile, seeded

1 tablespoon organic sugar

¼ teaspoon kosher salt

¼ cup sliced king trumpet mushroom stems, in ¼-inch-thick rounds

¼ cup halved cherry tomatoes

¼ cup sliced Japanese cucumber, in ¼-inch-thick half-moons

2 tablespoons paper-thin red radish slices, soaked in cold water for at least 1 hour to mellow the flavor, then drained

¼ cup diced red onion, in ¼-inch pieces

2 tablespoons finely chopped fresh cilantro stems

Kosher salt

¼ cup diced mango

¼ cup triangular-cut avocado, in ½-inch triangles

3-5 fresh cilantro sprigs for garnish

Corn tortilla chips of choice for serving

BRAISED BEET POKE

We've eaten boatloads of this poke and are still floored by its flavor. It tastes just like the sea and takes you straight to the beach, just as any poke should. It also looks exactly like the poke you'd get at one of those trendy quick-service restaurants. The color of the beets resembles fresh tuna, and by braising the beets, we tone down their earthiness and soften their texture, further adding to the similarity. The global tuna population is threatened by overfishing—in no small part due to the popularity of poke—and bycatch, and other bad practices. We hope something like this worthy, planet-friendly beet poke alternative starts to show up in restaurants all over the world.

THE PLAN: If you decide to make the togarashi, do that first. And toast the nuts if you don't have toasted nuts on hand. Then braise the beets for about 1 hour. While that's happening, prepare all the other components of the dish. Then all that's left to do is assemble and serve.

To cook the beets, combine the water, vinegar, and honey in a small stockpot and mix well. For the beets to cook evenly, the pot must be small enough for them to be completely submerged in the liquid. There must also be at least a few inches between the surface of the liquid and the pot rim so liquid does not boil over. If necessary, ladle out some of the liquid. Cover the pot with a lid or aluminum foil, place on the stove top over high heat, and bring to a boil. Reduce the heat to a simmer, cover, and braise the beets until a sharp knife or toothpick pierces easily to the center of a beet. The beets are usually ready in about 1¼ hours, but begin checking after 1 hour.

While the beets are cooking, make the sauce. In a small bowl, whisk together all the ingredients until well mixed and the sugar dissolves. You will need only 3 tablespoons sauce for the poke. Store the leftover sauce in an airtight container in the refrigerator for up to 1 month.

When the beets are ready, remove the pot from the stove top and let the beets continue to cook in the liquid. When the beets have cooled for about 20 minutes, don rubber gloves (to keep your hands from turning red) and remove the beets from the liquid. To skin each beet, wrap it in a paper towel and give it a gentle squeeze. The skin will slide off.

Once the beets are cool, cut them into ½-inch cubes. (Any scraps can be reserved for use in a salad or as a snack.) Measure out 2 cups cubed beets for the poke. Reserve the remainder for another use.

To assemble the poke, in a bowl, combine the beets, cucumber, avocado, radish, seaweed salad, and 3 tablespoons of the sauce and mix together very gently. Spoon the poke into the center of a serving bowl. Sprinkle with the nuts, green onions, and togarashi and serve with the rice crackers for scooping.

FOR THE BEETS

3 cups water

1 cup cider vinegar

½ cup Clover Blossom Honey (page 153) or packed brown sugar

2 lb medium red beets (as uniform in size as possible)

FOR THE SAUCE

⅓ cup raw cane, coconut, or date sugar

¼ cup fresh lemon juice

¼ cup mirin

¼ cup tamari

½ teaspoon toasted sesame oil

1 tablespoon extra-virgin olive oil (the nicer the better)

1 teaspoon peeled and grated fresh ginger

2-oz piece Japanese cucumber, sliced into ¼-inch-thick rounds

½ avocado, peeled and cut into ½-inch dice

2 watermelon radishes, peeled and shaved or thinly sliced

2 oz store-bought seaweed salad (about ⅓ cup)

½ cup macadamia nuts, toasted (see Note, page 33) and roughly chopped

1 tablespoon thinly sliced green onion, pale green parts only

1½ teaspoons togarashi, homemade (page 152) or store-bought

Rice crackers for serving (we like Japan's Clearspring brand puffed rice crackers)

GREEN FOREST FLATBREAD

We make this thin, cracker-like flatbread by stretching the dough completely by hand, but you can also use a rolling pin for a result that's a bit less bubbly. Blair tested every brand of plant-based cheese he could find before he deemed Violife shredded mozzarella the best for topping this flatbread because of the way it melts just like real cheese. He mixes it with some Miyoko's smoked mozzarella to add depth of flavor. The other toppings of mushrooms, broccolini, and arugula give this meal a just-healthy-enough, woodsy vibe.

 THE PLAN: Leave the dough at room temperature for 2 hours. Shape the dough, place it on the pizza peel, add the toppings, bake, and serve.

Remove the dough from the refrigerator. Oil a bowl, put the dough into it, cover the bowl tightly with plastic wrap, and let the dough proof again and come to room temperature for about 2 hours.

Position an oven rack in the upper third of the oven and place a pizza stone or an inverted sheet pan on the rack. Preheat the oven to 550°F. Give the pizza stone or sheet pan at least 20 minutes to get hot. (Pro tip: Blair likes to blast the pizza stone or sheet pan with the broiler for 5 minutes just before the pizza goes in. This increases the golden-brown crispiness factor on the bottom of the pizza crust.)

Zo shape the dough, first dust a pizza peel with the flour, then sprinkle with the cornmeal. (If you don't have a peel, a rimless cookie sheet, an upside-down sheet pan, or a large, stiff piece of cardboard will work.) Rub a work surface and your hands with about 1 tablespoon oil and put the dough on the surface. Flatten the ball into a thick disk with your hands or a few rolls of a rolling pin. Then, still using your hands or the rolling pin, push the disk from the center outward, working your way around the disk, to create a round 8-10 inches in diameter. Cover the dough with a clean kitchen towel and let rest for 5 minutes. Then, pick up the dough round and drape it over your two fists. Move your fists in a circular motion around the perimeter of the dough, allowing gravity to stretch the disk into a larger round. Once you have a 12-inch round, transfer the dough to the prepared peel.

Spread the chimichurri evenly over the dough all the way to the rim. Evenly sprinkle the shredded mozzarella on top. Then add the broccolini, mushrooms, and smoked cheese, distributing them evenly on top.

Slide the flatbread off the peel onto the pizza stone and bake, rotating the flatbread back to front halfway through baking, until the cheese is melted and the edges of the crust are golden brown, 5-7 minutes.

Just before the flatbread is ready, in a bowl, toss the arugula with the lemon juice, 1 teaspoon oil, and the salt. Then, using the pizza peel, retrieve the flatbread from the oven (you may need to use a spatula to shimmy it onto the peel) and transfer it to a cutting board. Distribute the dressed arugula evenly over the flatbread and brush any exposed crust edges with oil. Using a Y-shaped vegetable peeler, shave some Parmesan on top. Let the flatbread sit for 3 minutes before cutting and serving.

Pizza Dough (page 167)

1 tablespoon "00" flour

1 tablespoon yellow cornmeal

Extra-virgin olive oil as needed

¼ cup chimichurri (see Marinated Feta with Chimichurri, page 150)

½ cup Violife shredded mozzarella cheese

½ cup cut-up grilled broccolini, in 2-inch pieces

½ cup torn chanterelle or oyster mushrooms, in bite-size pieces

3 oz Miyoko's smoked mozzarella cheese, cut into ½-inch pieces

½ cup loosely packed arugula

½ teaspoon fresh lemon juice

Pinch of kosher salt

Wedge of Violife plant-based Parmesan cheese for finishing

MAKE IT A WHITE TRUFFLE PIZZA: For a slightly richer flavor profile, substitute truffled ricotta for the chimichurri. To make truffled ricotta, mix together ½ cup plant-based ricotta cheese, preferably Miyoko's brand; 1 tablespoon truffle butter, homemade (page 160) or store-bought; ½ teaspoon truffle oil, and ¼ teaspoon kosher salt. Reduce the amount of Violife mozzarella ricotta on the dough in place of the chimichurri, then proceed as directed in the recipe.

FRENCH ONION DIP
WITH VEGETABLE CHIPS

This simple dip is one of the best-selling bar snacks at Wildseed. It's on every table during happy hour and with good reason. We made our own chips at the restaurant, but for your purposes, go with store-bought. We love Terra brand chips in the Warsham household, but it seems a new vegetable chip emerges on the market shelves every day, so feel free to sample different brands. Freeze-dried vegetables, such as okra and lotus root, are another nice addition to the chip bowl. Caramelizing the onions is critical to the success of this recipe, so take your time with that step.

 THE PLAN: Caramelize the onions. Combine them with the remaining dip ingredients. Cut the chives, garnish, and eat!

In a large sauté pan, heat the oil over medium heat. Add the onions and season well with salt. (The oil should be hot enough to create a little sizzle when the onions are added.) Immediately turn down the heat to medium-low or low to allow the onions to caramelize very slowly. Stir the onions often as they cook, adding a few tablespoons of water if they begin to stick to the pan. They are finished when the color is deep brown, like French onion soup. This should take about 15 minutes. Spread the cooked onions on a sheet pan and let cool completely.

In a bowl, combine the cooled onions, sour cream, Worcestershire sauce, and onion and garlic powders and mix well. Taste and adjust the seasoning with salt if needed.

Top the dip with the chives and serve with the chips.

2 tablespoons extra-virgin olive oil

2 cups finely diced yellow onions, in ⅛-inch dice (2 small or 1 large onion)

Kosher salt

2 cups Tofutti sour cream

2 tablespoons plant-based Worcestershire sauce

½ teaspoon onion powder

½ teaspoon garlic powder

1 tablespoon very finely sliced fresh chives

Vegetable chips of choice for serving

PAN PIZZA WITH PEPPERS, ONIONS & SAUSAGE

Blair and I both grew up eating Pizza Hut's personal pepperoni pan pizzas. Now we can have plant-based pepper pan pizza, which also rolls right off the tongue. This thick crust's combination of crispy exterior and doughy middle takes me back to those school-night dinners when I just wanted to linger over my personal pepperoni pan pizza all night so I didn't have to go home and do homework. Another nice thing about this recipe is that you can make it in a cast-iron skillet.

THE PLAN: Leave the dough at room temperature for 2 hours. Make the pizza sauce. Press the dough into the cast-iron pan and add the toppings. Cook the pizza on the stove top for a few minutes and then bake it in the oven.

Remove the dough from the refrigerator. Oil a bowl, put the dough into it, cover the bowl tightly with plastic wrap, and let the dough proof again and come to room temperature for about 2 hours.

Meanwhile, make the sauce. Select a small, heavy pot with a lid. Heat the oil in the pot over high heat. When oil is smoking hot, add the garlic and let cook for a few seconds. Then add the tomatoes and juice and immediately cover the pot. Let the tomatoes bubble violently for a few seconds, then reduce the heat to a simmer. Uncover and add the salt, oregano, paprika (if using), and pepper flakes. Stir well, re-cover, and let the sauce simmer for 35 minutes to blend the flavors. Remove from the heat, then taste and add the sugar if needed to balance the acidity. Let the sauce cool to room temperature. Measure out ½ cup sauce for the pizza. The leftover sauce will keep in an airtight container in the refrigerator for up to 1 week.

Preheat the oven to 450°F. Brush a 10-inch cast-iron frying pan with the oil. Transfer the dough directly to the center of the pan. Using your fingers, press the dough across the bottom and up the sides of the pan to the rim. It's best to do this in two stages, allowing the dough to rest at the halfway point for about 5 minutes.

Spread the ½ cup pizza sauce evenly over the dough all the way to the rim. Evenly sprinkle the Violife mozzarella on top. Add the sausage, onion, pepper, and smoked mozzarella in even layers on top, then season with salt.

Turn on a stove-top burner to medium heat, set the pan on the burner, and leave to heat for 2 minutes. You will not see much action here, but this step helps to brown the bottom of the crust. Now transfer the pan to the oven and bake the pizza, rotating the pan back to front about halfway through baking, until the cheese is melted and the edges of the crust are golden brown, 10–15 minutes.

Remove from the oven and let rest for 1 minute. Using a spatula, loosen the edges of the pizza and transfer to a cutting board.

Using a Microplane or other fine-rasp grater, grate some Parmesan on top, then let sit for 3 minutes. Drizzle with the oil just before cutting and serving.

Pizza Dough (page 167) or 6 oz store-bought pizza dough

Olive oil for the bowl

FOR THE SAUCE

2 tablespoons olive oil

1½ tablespoons thinly sliced garlic

1 can (14 oz) diced or crushed San Marzano tomatoes with juice

½ teaspoon kosher salt

½ teaspoon fresh or dried oregano

½ teaspoon smoked paprika (optional)

¼ teaspoon red pepper flakes

½ teaspoon organic sugar if needed

1 tablespoon olive oil

1 cup Violife shredded mozzarella cheese

1 Beyond Sausage spicy Italian sausage, cut into ¼-inch-thick rounds

½ cup thinly sliced red onion

¼ cup thinly sliced red bell pepper

3 tablespoons cubed Miyoko's smoked mozzarella cheese, in ½-inch cubes

Kosher salt

Wedge of Violife plant-based Parmesan cheese for finishing

2 tablespoons extra-virgin olive oil for finishing

BLAIR'S SOUTHERN BARBECUE
DINNER PLATTER

Barbecue has always been kind of a scary word for plant-based eaters,
but here's a backyard grill fest made entirely from plants (See image spread, page
104–105.) Start with fresh-grilled vegetables and sausages, creamy potatoes,
cooling smashed cucumbers, and juicy watermelon salad. Now add your
Southern flair with corn bread, Alabama white sauce, and grilled peaches for dessert.

Barbecue-Grilled Vegetables & Beyond Sausage (page 60)
Roasted Marble Potatoes with Black Garlic & Charred Green Onion Aioli (page 80)
Smashed Cucumbers with Sesame, Cilantro & Vinegar (page 79)
10-Minute Watermelon, Cucumber & Basil Salad (page 34)
Weeknight Corn Bread (page 84) and Truffle Butter (page 160)
Alabama White Sauce (page 166)
Pickled Onions (page 154)
Grilled Peaches & Ice Cream (page 130)

Breakfast

APPLE PANCAKES WITH MAPLE, ROASTED PECANS & COCONUT WHIPPED CREAM

We're not going to dance around it: this is our favorite pancake hack. The recipe uses a commercial mix to achieve a restaurant-quality breakfast: caramelized apple–filled pancakes, toasty pecans, steaming maple syrup, airy whipped coconut cream. It's one of our easier recipes, but it didn't come together without effort. We tested every vegan-friendly pancake mix we could find, and we like the Birch Benders plant protein mix the best. Why? It yields a fluffy, springy, protein-loaded cake with a nice brown sear on the outside. Plus, you won't be hungry a few hours later! If you cannot find Birch Benders where you are, order it online or use the pancake mix you like.

 THE PLAN: If using homemade coconut whipped cream, make it first, then toast the nuts. Cut and caramelize the apples. Make the batter. Make pancakes!

Heat a large sauté pan over medium heat. Add 1 tablespoon of the butter and allow it to melt and then foam. Add the apples, season with ¼ teaspoon of the salt, and cook the apples undisturbed for about 1 minute to achieve some caramelization. Then continue to cook, stirring as little as possible, until tender and somewhat caramelized, 4–7 minutes. The more you move the apples the less they will caramelize. That said, keep an eye on them, as you don't want them to burn. Remove the pan from the heat, add the maple syrup, stir to mix, and transfer to a bowl. Cover to keep warm.

To make the pancake batter, put the mix into a bowl and, following the directions on the package, add the water. Then mix in half of the apple mixture, the baking powder, vanilla, vinegar, the remaining ¼ teaspoon salt, and the melted butter, if using. The melted butter helps keep the pancakes from sticking, but you can skip it.

Heat a griddle or large frying pan over medium-high heat. The pan is hot enough when water flicked onto the surface sizzles and evaporates on contact. If using a cast-iron pan, keep an eye on the heat throughout cooking, as cast iron holds heat especially well and you may need to turn down the heat.

Add about 1 tablespoon oil to the pan, then, using a paper towel, quickly spread it around and wipe off the excess. For each pancake, using a ¼-cup measuring cup, scoop up the batter and pour it into the pan, cooking 1–3 pancakes at a time, depending on the size of your pan. Cook until bubbles form and pop on the surface and the edges are mostly dry, 1–2 minutes, then flip the pancakes over and cook for 1 minute longer. As the pancakes are ready, transfer them directly to individual serving plates. Repeat with the remaining batter, adding more oil to the pan as needed to prevent sticking.

To serve, top the pancakes with the remaining apple-maple mixture, a sprinkle of pecans, and a dollop of coconut cream.

2 tablespoons Miyoko's unsalted butter, plus 2 tablespoons, melted (optional)

2 cups peeled, cored, and diced Pink Lady or other tart-sweet apples, in ½-inch dice

½ teaspoon kosher salt

¼ cup plus 3 tablespoons pure maple syrup

1 bag (14 oz) Birch Benders plant protein pancake mix

2 ¼ cups water or plant-based milk

1 teaspoon baking powder

1 tablespoon pure vanilla extract

1 teaspoon cider vinegar

Rice bran oil for cooking

½ cup pecans, toasted (see Note, page 33)

Coconut whipped cream, homemade (page 142) or store-bought

BANANA FRITTERS WITH CHOCOLATE-HAZELNUT SAUCE

If you have been looking for an excuse to eat a healthyish doughnut for breakfast, look no further than these doughnut-like fritters. Blair had Nutella on the brain when he created this dish. Nutella is a sugary, Italian-made chocolate-hazelnut spread that's popular all over the world. It's also amazing with bananas. Since it's made with whey and milk, we're happy to say that a number of fantastic plant-based substitutes exist. Justin's, Nutiva, Rawmio, and Artisana are among our favorite brands.

You will need a stand mixer with a dough hook to make the dough. This is a super-fun weekend breakfast project—great for lazy mornings when you can watch cartoons while the dough rises.

 THE PLAN: Make the dough and let it rise for an hour. Then heat the oil, fry the fritters, and serve hot.

In the bowl of a stand mixer fitted with the dough hook, combine the water, yeast, salt, and egg replacer and beat on low speed until mixed. In a bowl, sift together the all-purpose and rice flours while you wait 3–4 minutes for the yeast to wake up. Then add the sifted flours to the yeast mixxture and mix on low speed until a soft and sticky dough forms, about 3 minutes. Add the hemp hearts and bananas and mix on low speed until incorporated, about 1 minute. Remove the bowl from the mixer stand, cover with plastic wrap, and find a warm place for the dough to proof for 1 hour. It will roughly double in size.

Pour the oil to a depth of 2–3 inches into a deep, heavy pot and heat to 350°F on a deep-frying thermometer (see Note, page 70). Line a large plate generously with paper towels and set it near the stove.

Now set the bowl of dough near the stove. Using a 1-oz ice-cream or similar-size scoop or cup, drop scoopfuls of the dough into the hot oil, being careful not to crowd the pot. Fry the fritters until they rise to the top and are browned on all sides, 4–6 minutes. Use tongs to turn the fritters as they cook to ensure they brown evenly. Using a wire skimmer or slotted spoon, transfer the fritters to the towel-lined plate to drain. Repeat frying in batches until all the dough is used up.

If desired, put several spoonfuls of powdered sugar into a shallow bowl. While the fritters are warm (not hot), add them, a few at a time, to the sugar and turn them to coat evenly.

Serve the fritters right away with the chocolate-hazelnut spread on the side for dipping and spreading. If you're feeling fancy, smear ¼ cup of the chocolate-hazelnut spread onto each individual serving plate and arrange the fritters on top before serving.

FOR THE DOUGH

2 ¼ cups body-temperature water (95°–100°F)

2 ½ teaspoons active dry yeast

1 teaspoon kosher salt

2 tablespoons Bob's Red Mill Egg Replacer, prepared for 2 whole eggs according to package directions

3 cups all-purpose flour

½ cup superfine rice flour or cornstarch

½ cup hemp hearts

2 cups sliced banana

Rice bran or vegetable oil for deep-frying

Organic powdered sugar for dusting (optional)

1 cup plant-based chocolate-hazelnut spread

SMOKED CARROT
& CREAM CHEESE TARTINE

Here, we slowly cook the carrots until they get as close to smoked salmon as they're ever going to get. The texture becomes velvety and the flavor is deeply savory. Blair has a lot of mixed feelings about creating mock meat—especially from vegetables. If it's good enough to eat by itself, then it passes the test. This smoked carrot is indeed delicious on its own, but we're taking inspiration from the delis of America by serving it with cream cheese, dill, and capers.

 THE PLAN: Cook the carrots low and slow. Then cool and assemble the toast.

To make the smoked carrot, trim the carrots, then scrub them with warm water. You do not need to peel them. Cut the carrots crosswise into 3-inch-long logs. Then, using a mandoline or sharp chef's knife, cut the logs lengthwise into ⅛-inch-thick planks.

Pour the water into a pot and bring to a boil over high heat. Add the carrots to the boiling water and parboil until half cooked, 2–5 minutes. Scoop the carrots out of the water and transfer them to a large resealable plastic bag.

Add the coconut aminos, tamari, liquid smoke, sugar, and lemon and lime zests to the bag and mix well to coat the carrots evenly. Seal the bag with either a vacuum sealer or using the Ziploc bag method described in the sidebar.

Place the pot on the stove top over high heat and heat the water to 185°F on an instant-read thermometer, adjusting the heat as needed to maintain the temperature. Submerge the bag in the water and use a weight to keep it in place.

Cook the carrots for 1½ hours at 185°F, checking the temperature regularly and adjusting the heat if needed to meet the target temperature. Just before the carrots are ready, fill a large bowl with water and ice. When the carrots are cooked, transfer the bag to the ice bath and let cool completely.

The carrots are now ready to use, or they can be refrigerated in the marinade in the bag for up to 1 week. You will need only about one-fourth of the carrots for this recipe. When ready to serve, open the bag, remove enough carrot planks to cover the tartines generously, give them a gentle rinse under cold water, and pat dry with paper towels.

To assemble the tartines, toast the bread either in a toaster or brush with oil and toast on a grill. Spread each toast slice with half of the cream cheese. Top the cream cheese with carrot curls by twisting each plank into a snake-like curl and propping it up on its skinny edge. Then, add the dill, tomatoes, onion, and capers and serve.

THE ZIPLOC BAG SOUS VIDE METHOD: Place the item you want to cook into a Ziploc or other sturdy resealable plastic bag and leave the top of the bag open. Fill a container with water and slowly lower the open bag into the water-filled container, keeping the top of the bag above the water line. The pressure of the water will force the air up and out the top of the bag. When the portion of the bag with the food is fully submerged, carefully seal the bag above the water line. Once you begin cooking, place a weight on the bag to keep it submerged.

FOR THE SMOKED CARROT

1 lb jumbo carrots

About 6 cups water

¼ cup coconut aminos

¼ cup tamari

½ teaspoon liquid smoke

2 tablespoons organic sugar

Grated zest of 2 lemons

Grated zest of 2 limes

2 large slices rye or seeded bread

Olive oil if grilling bread

¼ cup Miyoko's cream cheese

2 tablespoons small fresh dill sprigs

½ cup sliced cherry tomatoes

2 tablespoons shaved red onion or Pickled Onions (page 154)

1 tablespoon drained capers

GRILLED AVOCADO TOAST

By now, we're sure you are well acquainted with avocado toast. But have you ever had it on grilled sourdough bread? When you throw extra-thick slices of naturally leavened bread like pain au levain on the grill before topping them with avocado, a whole new level is added to the flavor profile. Warning: this recipe may ruin you forever for regular avocado toast.

While we've put this in the Breakfast chapter, grilled avocado toast never met a meal or time of day it didn't fit perfectly.

 THE PLAN: Prep all the ingredients. Grill the bread and assemble the toasts.

Prepare the grill for indirect cooking over medium-high heat. Brush each bread slice on both sides with oil, using 1 tablespoon oil for each side. Season both sides of each slice with a pinch of kosher salt.

Place the bread next to the flames on the cooler side of the grill. (You can gauge the heat by holding your hand roughly a foot above the grill to feel for hot spots; do not grill the bread directly over the flames.) Grill the slices, turning them twice during cooking, until grill marks are pronounced on both sides and the bread is golden brown, about 5 minutes total.

Transfer the bread to a work surface and immediately divide the cheese between the slices, spooning it onto the center of each slice. Spread the cheese toward the edges, leaving a ½-inch border on all edges.

Halve and pit the avocado. Spoon the flesh in one piece from each half and place the halves, cut side down, on a cutting board. Slice each half horizontally a few times and then, using the back of a fork, gently press the avocado flat. Using a knife or spatula, lift each avocado half and set it on the center of a toast. Drizzle the toasts with the remaining 2 tablespoons oil and the lemon juice, dividing them evenly. Finally, top each toast with a little sea salt and half each of the lemon zest, pickled onions, and za'atar. Eat it while it's hot!

2 slices double-thick-cut pain au levain (sourdough bread), each about 1 inch thick

6 tablespoons extra-virgin olive oil

Kosher salt

6 tablespoons plant-based ricotta cheese, preferably Kite Hill brand

1 avocado

Juice of 1 lemon

Maldon sea salt

Grated zest of ½ lemon

2 tablespoons Pickled Onions (page 154)

1 tablespoon za'atar

SAVORY ONE-POT OATMEAL
WITH CHARD, THYME & TOFU

This is our go-to camping breakfast because it's fragrant, nourishing, warm, and comes together in one pan over a campfire. Of course, it's even easier to make at home on your stove top. Like many of our recipes, the carbs don't dominate. Instead, this dish is a goldmine of all sorts of delicious vegetables and protein. Most people expect oatmeal to be served with sweet ingredients, so this savory gem is an eye-opener. Peppers, asparagus, and avocado make great additions to this one-pan meal.

 THE PLAN: Cut up the vegetables, then make the oatmeal in one pot, building layers of flavor as you go.

Heat a 2-quart cast-iron pan or similar vessel over medium heat. (The pan must be large enough to hold everything without overcrowding.) Add the butter and let it foam and brown for about 1 minute. Add onion and sweat, stirring occasionally, for 1 minute.

Increase the heat to high, add the mushrooms, chard, and garlic and cook, stirring until you see a little color on the mushrooms and the garlic begins to cook but not burn, 1-2 minutes. Add the stock base, water, tomatoes, tofu, oats, thyme, and salt and stir well to incorporate all the ingredients. Reduce the heat to medium-low, cover, and simmer, stirring occasionally, until the oatmeal is cooked and the vegetables are tender, about 10 minutes.

Remove from the heat and scatter the goat cheese over the top, if using. Serve the oatmeal directly from the pan.

2 tablespoons Miyoko's unsalted butter

1 cup julienned red onion

1 cup cremini or other mushrooms, brushed clean and cut into 1-inch pieces

1 cup packed stemmed torn or cut Swiss chard or kale leaves

3 cloves garlic, minced

1 teaspoon Better Than Bouillon no chicken base

1 cup water

½ cup cherry or other small tomatoes

1 cup cubed smoked or braised tofu, in 1-inch cubes

1 cup Bob's Red Mill quick-cooking steel-cut oats

4-6 fresh thyme sprigs

1 teaspoon kosher salt

¼ cup crumbled Spero goat cheese (optional)

VANILLA CHIA PUDDING
WITH ROASTED STRAWBERRY SAUCE

Chia seeds have a gazillion health benefits. They are high in fiber, omega-3 fatty acids, protein, antioxidants, and the list goes on. You can eat this chia pudding as a nutritious breakfast or scale down the portion size for dessert. The chia seeds will taste best if you let them absorb all the other ingredients overnight in the refrigerator, but you might be impatient. It'll still taste delicious even if you eat it just an hour after mixing.

This recipe calls for a homemade strawberry jam that is impressive and easy to make. Feel free to substitute other fresh fruits (see the sidebar for ideas). We especially like the pudding with passion fruit purée, which you can order online.

 THE PLAN: Soak the chia seeds and other pudding ingredients for as long as you can wait. Make the jam. Top the pudding with the granola, yogurt, and jam and serve.

To make the pudding, in a bowl, whisk together the chia seeds, milk, sugar, vanilla, salt, and cinnamon (if using). Let stand until you see the seeds begin to rehydrate, about 5 minutes, then whisk again very well. Chia pudding easily lumps, so be sure to whisk it several more times while the seeds are soaking up all of the other goodness. Cover the bowl and refrigerate the pudding for at least 1 hour or up to overnight.

To make the jam, preheat the oven to 175°F. Hull the strawberries, quarter them lengthwise, and drop them into a bowl. Add the sugar, star anise, and salt and toss well. Turn the berries out into a large baking dish and spread them out.

Roast the berries, stirring them occasionally, until they release some of their liquid and begin to cook, about 15 minutes.

Transfer the berries to a food processor and pulse twice to achieve a jam-like consistency. Let cool, then refrigerate in an airtight container until needed.

To plate the pudding, add a touch of milk to the pudding and whisk a bit to break up the blob that it has likely become while chilling in the refrigerator. Divide the pudding evenly between individual serving bowls. Sprinkle ½ cup of the granola around the rim of each bowl, then spoon ½ cup of the yogurt into the center of each bowl. Top each mound of yogurt with ½ cup of the jam and serve.

FOR THE PUDDING
½ cup chia seeds

1 ½ cups almond, oat, coconut, or other nondairy milk

1 tablespoon date or coconut sugar

1 teaspoon vanilla paste, or seeds from 1 vanilla bean

¼ teaspoon kosher salt

¼ teaspoon ground cinnamon (optional)

FOR THE JAM
1 lb strawberries

2 tablespoons date or coconut sugar

Pinch of ground star anise

¼ teaspoon kosher salt

FOR SERVING
Additional nondairy milk as needed to thin

1 cup favorite sweet granola

1 cup nondairy vanilla coconut yogurt

A FEW MORE GREAT CHIA PUDDING IDEAS:

Blueberry nut: Omit the jam. Layer almond butter over the chia pudding. Garnish with fresh blueberries and nutty granola.

Coco banana: Omit the jam. Whisk 1 tablespoon high-quality unsweetened cocoa powder into the chia pudding as you are making it. Layer banana slices on top. Garnish with sea salt, cacao nibs, and toasted dried coconut.

Peaches and cream: Substitute peaches for the strawberries and ginger for the star anise in the jam. Layer fresh peach slices on top of the jam and garnish with fennel pollen.

GREEN GODDESS SCRAMBLE
WITH KALE & BLISTERED TOMATOES

A classic invented in San Francisco in the early twentieth century, green goddess dressing—a blend of mayonnaise, olive oil, sour cream, several different herbs, and anchovies—has a very light tasting, yet rich flavor—sort of like a pumped-up version of ranch. Here, we layer a similar flavor profile into plant-based eggs with some greens and other vegetables and finish it off with a dollop of plant-based sour cream. The result is a healthy scramble that's full of interest and just enough indulgence to taste great.

THE PLAN: Mix the egg with the seasonings and then cook the vegetables. Clean the pan and cook the eggs a bit before returning the vegetables to the pan to finish. In a bowl, whisk together the egg, chives, tarragon, salt, and a turn or two of the pepper mill and set aside until ready to cook.

In a sauté pan, heat 1 tablespoon of the oil over high heat until smoking. Add the cherry tomatoes and cook until the skins have blistered and are beginning to come off, about 2 minutes. Transfer to a plate.

Add the remaining 1 tablespoon oil to the same pan and place over medium-high heat. Add the red onion and cook, stirring, until soft, about 2 minutes. Add the kale and arugula and cook, tossing occasionally, until the greens are wilted and any liquid has evaporated, 2–3 minutes. Transfer the vegetables to the plate with the tomatoes and wipe out the pan.

Return the pan to medium-high heat and melt the butter. Add the egg mixture and cook, stirring slowly but constantly with a silicone spatula, until barely set, about 1 minute. Return all the vegetables to the pan and gently fold them into the egg. Continue cooking until the egg is just set, 1–2 minutes.

Divide the scramble evenly between individual serving plates, spoon 1 tablespoon of the sour cream onto the center of each portion, and serve.

2 tablespoons extra-virgin olive oil

½ cup cherry tomatoes (the smaller the better)

¼ cup julienned red onion

1 cup loosely packed baby kale

1 cup loosely packed arugula

1 teaspoon Miyoko's unsalted butter

1 cup Just Egg

2 tablespoons thinly sliced fresh chives

1 tablespoon chopped fresh tarragon leaves

¼ teaspoon kosher salt

Freshly ground black pepper

2 tablespoons Tofutti sour cream

SAVORY FRENCH TOAST WITH HOLLANDAISE & SEASONAL VEGETABLES

Savory French toast is a brilliant idea, and this version makes the genre proud. Having trained in France early in his career, Blair decided that making an amazing plant-based hollandaise was his hill to die on. After testing this hollandaise more then twenty times, he hit a winner. Himalayan black salt (kala namak) is the key. It has an interesting flavor profile, smells like hard-boiled eggs, has so many health benefits that it's used in Ayurvedic medicine, and adds a heavy dose of umami to dishes. You're going to want to put it on everything you eat—rice, pasta, vegetables, beans, and more.

 THE PLAN: Soak and brown the toast. Then make the hollandaise, cook the toppings, and assemble the dish.

Preheat the oven to its lowest setting. To make the toast, select a bowl just large enough to fit a bread slice and to hold the egg mixture. Pour the egg and water into the bowl, add the salt, and mix well. Place a bread slice in the liquid and let sit for 2-5 minutes to soak up the goodness. Transfer to a plate. Repeat with the remaining bread slices.

Lightly grease a large frying pan with neutral oil and heat over medium heat. Working in batches, add the soaked bread slices to the hot pan and cook, turning once, until browned on both sides, 1-2 minutes on each side. Transfer to a sheet pan and keep warm in the oven.

To make the hollandaise, cut the butter into ½-inch cubes, put it into a bowl, and put the bowl into the freezer while you get everything else together. In a second bowl, whisk together the stock, hot sauce, cornstarch, miso, salt, and turmeric until the cornstarch dissolves.

Pour the stock mixture into a small saucepan and bring to a simmer over medium heat. Begin whisking in the butter cubes, one piece at a time, whisking continuously to create an emulsion. When all the butter is emulsified into the stock mixture, remove from the heat and whisk in the mayonnaise and lemon juice. Transfer to a small heatproof container and cover to keep warm.

To prepare the toppings, heat a large sauté pan over high heat for 1 minute. Meanwhile, line a plate with a paper towel. Add the mushrooms to the dry pan and sprinkle them with ¼ teaspoon of the salt. Sauté until cooked through, 1-2 minutes, depending on the size and density. Transfer the mushrooms to the towel-lined plate.

Return the pan to medium-high heat and add the oil. When the oil is hot, add the onion and the remaining ¼ teaspoon salt and cook, stirring, until the onion begins to color, about 1 minute. Add the chard and stir with the onion until it begins to wilt. Then cover the pan and remove from the heat. The vegetables will finish cooking in the carryover heat and the steam.

Divide the toasts between two individual serving plates. Gently spoon one-fourth each of the mushrooms, chard, and any of the optional toppings, if using, onto each toast. Cover the toasts with a small blanket of warm hollandaise and serve.

FOR THE TOAST

2 cups Just Egg

1 cup water

¼ teaspoon kosher salt

4 large, thick-cut slices favorite seeded bread, about 1 inch thick

Neutral oil, such as rich bran or avocado, for cooking

FOR THE HOLLANDAISE

4 tablespoons Miyoko's unsalted butter

¼ cup Better than Bouillon no chicken stock

2-4 dashes hot sauce (Tapatío or your favorite brand)

1½ teaspoons cornstarch

½ teaspoon white (shiro) miso

⅛ teaspoon Himalayan black salt

⅛ teaspoon ground turmeric

2 tablespoons Just Mayo

½ teaspoon fresh lemon juice

FOR THE TOPPINGS

2 cups cut or torn maitake or other mushrooms of choice, in bite-size pieces

½ teaspoon kosher salt

2 tablespoons olive oil

1 cup julienned red onion

4 cups stemmed then cut chard leaves, in 1-inch pieces

Seared cherry tomatoes, cubed smoked tofu, and/or julienned roasted red peppers (optional)

RED SALSA CHILAQUILES WITH AVOCADO & EGGS

On Sundays at Wildseed, these chilaquiles were on nearly every table at brunch. A crowd-pleasing Mexican breakfast dish, chilaquiles consists of tortilla chips that are soaked in flavorful tomato sauce and then topped with sour cream and cheese. We serve our version with plenty of spicy pico de gallo, eggs, and avocado. They're a great shareable brunch snack and also an entirely respectable main dish.

THE PLAN: Make the pico de gallo and salsa, then finish up cutting any remaining ingredients. Cook the eggs and Soyrizo (if using), toss the chips in the red salsa, plate, and garnish.

To make the pico de gallo, neatly dice the tomatoes, onion, and chile as directed. Take care with the cutting, as uniform pieces make for a better eating experience. If you want some guidance on cutting, read the sidebar. In a bowl, combine the tomatoes, onion, chile, cilantro, and lime juice, toss to mix, and season to taste with sea salt. Measure 1 cup for the chilaquiles and set aside. Store any leftover salsa in an airtight container in the refrigerator for up to 1 week.

To make the red salsa, pour 4 cups of the water into a small saucepan and bring to a boil over high heat. While the water is heating, stem the chiles and put the chiles and onion into a heatproof bowl. Carefully pour the boiling water into the bowl, then stir the chiles and onion to make sure they are evenly saturated. Cover the bowl with a large plate, aluminum foil, or plastic wrap and let the mixture soak until softened, about 15 minutes.

Using a slotted spoon, transfer the softened chiles and onion to a blender. Add the tomatoes, garlic, olive oil, salt, and the remaining ¾ cup water and purée until completely smooth. Measure 1 cup salsa for the chilaquiles. Store the remainder in an airtight container in the refrigerator for up to 1 week.

In a nonstick frying pan, heat 1 tablespoon of the neutral oil over high heat. When the oil is hot, add the egg and cook, stirring, just until set, about 1 minute. Transfer to a plate. If using the Soyrizo, clean the pan, return it to medium-high heat, and add the remaining 1 tablespoon oil. Cook, stirring, for a few minutes until browned. Remove from the heat.

Put the chips into a large bowl, add the 1 cup red salsa, toss well, and then let sit for 1 minute so the salsa soaks into the chips. Using a slotted spoon, transfer the chips to a large serving bowl or individual serving bowls. Top with the 1 cup pico de gallo, the egg, Soyrizo (if using), sour cream, avocado, cheese (if using), and cilantro and serve.

HOW TO DICE: Blair does not like to use the word chop for cutting most vegetables, because it evokes the reckless use of a hatchet striking down with great force. In contrast, dicing vegetables is a precise action. For a round vegetable like a tomato, begin by cutting the vegetable in half horizontally. Then place the halves cut side down on a cutting board. Starting at the top of each half and cutting parallel to the board, cut into slabs ¼ inch thick. Next, holding the tomato slabs together, cut them into ¼-inch-wide sticks. Finally, cut the sticks crosswise into ¼-inch dice. This method can be used for most vegetables.

FOR THE PICO DE GALLO

2-3 ripe plum tomatoes (about ¾ lb), seeded and cut into ¼-inch dice

⅓ cup diced white onion, in ¼-inch dice

1 serrano chile, seeded and cut into ¼-inch dice

2 tablespoons roughly chopped fresh cilantro leaves and stems

2 tablespoons fresh lime juice

Sea salt

FOR THE RED SALSA

4 ¾ cups water

¼ oz dried árbol chiles (about 6)

¼ cup coarsely diced white onion

2 plum tomatoes, halved

2 cloves garlic

1 tablespoon extra-virgin olive oil

½ teaspoon kosher salt

1-2 tablespoons neutral oil, such as rice bran or avocado

¾ cup Just Egg

1 cup Soyrizo (soy-based chorizo) removed from casing (optional)

4 cups tortilla chips, preferably Xochitl or other high-quality Mexican brand

¼ cup Tofutti sour cream

1 avocado, halved, pitted, peeled, and diced

¼ cup Violife shredded mozzarella cheese (optional)

Fresh cilantro sprigs, torn into bite-size pieces, for garnish

EASY CARROT CAKE OATS

Our whole family is obsessed with carrot cake to the point that it's almost always our cake (or cupcake) of choice come birthday time. This recipe brings that birthday cake feeling to the breakfast table. If you love carrot cake as much as we do, this will brighten your morning routine.

THE PLAN: Mix the oats with the spices and other ingredients. Refrigerate for at least 6 hours. Add the toppings and serve.

In a bowl, combine the almond milk, oats, carrot, sugar, vanilla, cinnamon, nutmeg, salt, and 1 tablespoon each of the pecans and raisins and stir to mix well. Pour into a wide-mouthed Mason jar or other widemouthed container (it needs to be wide so it's easy to add the toppings) with a lid. Cover and refrigerate for at least 6 hours and ideally for 12 hours.

Remove from the refrigerator, uncover, top with the remaining 1 tablespoon each pecans and raisins, the coconut, and the coconut whipped cream, and serve.

YOUR OVERNIGHT OAT KIT: If you really take a liking to this recipe, you can quadruple the dry ingredients and have them all waiting together in a holding pattern for an evening when you'd like to anticipate having carrot cake for breakfast. This way, before bed, all you have to do is scoop ½ cup of the dry mix into a Mason jar, stir in the carrots, vanilla bean paste, and milk and then refrigerate overnight.

⅔ cup unsweetened vanilla almond milk

⅓ cup Bob's Red Mill quick-cooking steel-cut oats

¼ cup shredded carrot

1 tablespoon coconut sugar

¼ teaspoon vanilla bean paste

⅛ teaspoon ground cinnamon

Pinch of freshly grated nutmeg

Pinch of kosher salt

2 tablespoons pecans, toasted (see Note, page 33)

2 tablespoons raisins or other dried fruit of choice chopped roughly to the size of raisins

1 tablespoon unsweetened shredded dried coconut, toasted (optional)

1 tablespoon coconut whipped cream, homemade (page 142) or store-bought

Desserts

WHIPPED BANANA SUNDAE

There's a "health-minded" place called the Bashful Banana on the boardwalk in Ocean City, New Jersey, that has been serving banana whip since 2009. We travel to the Jersey Shore to see family every summer, so stopping for a banana whip is an expected part of our hot-weather routine.

What's banana whip, you ask? It's a banana that is juiced until it resembles soft-serve ice cream. That's it, and the texture is amazing. And if you don't have a juicer, you can use a high-speed blender or a food processor (though the latter does not work quite as well).

Here, we turn banana whip into a classic-style sundae by crowning it with chocolate sauce, nuts, cherries, and coconut whipped cream. Of course, the sky is the limit when it comes to toppings.

 THE PLAN: Freeze the bananas, toast the nuts, make the chocolate sauce, then make the whip.

Peel the bananas, cut into 1-inch pieces, drop the pieces into a plastic bag, and freeze for at least 2 hours.

To make the chocolate sauce, in a small saucepan, whisk together the water, sugar, agave nectar, and cocoa powder over medium heat. When the mixture begins to boil, immediately remove it from the heat and stir in the chocolate pieces until melted. Set aside until ready to use. It will thicken over the 2 hours the bananas are in the freezer. You need only ½ cup sauce for this recipe. The leftover sauce will keep in an airtight container in the refrigerator for up to 2 months.

Put the frozen bananas into a juicer, high-speed blender, or food processor and process until the mixture looks mousse-like and creamy. It will look lumpy and quite messy at first, but do not despair. After a minute or two, the bananas will magically transform into a creamy, whipped texture. This is what you want! Watch it closely and stop the moment you achieve the correct consistency.

Scoop the banana whip directly into individual serving bowls. Top each bowl with ¼ cup of the chocolate sauce, followed by the pistachios, cherries, and whipped cream, dividing them evenly. Finish with a dusting of sprinkles, if using, and serve.

IF YOU WANT TO GET FANCY: To take your banana whip presentation up a notch, scoop the whipped frozen banana into a resealable plastic bag and refreeze it for about 15 minutes. Cut a 1-inch hole in a bottom corner of the bag. Now, to make the banana whip look like soft serve, pipe it into the serving bowls in a circular motion by applying pressure to the top of the bag with your dominant hand. *Et voilà.* You're fancy.

2 bananas

FOR THE CHOCOLATE SAUCE

1 cup water

½ cup organic sugar

½ cup agave nectar

¾ cup high-quality unsweetened cocoa powder or cacao powder

2 oz high-quality dark or semisweet chocolate, such as Theo or Hu brand, finely chopped

FOR THE TOPPINGS

¼ cup pistachio nuts, toasted (see Note, page 33)

¼ cup brandied cherries

½ cup coconut whipped cream, homemade (page 142) or store-bought

Chocolate sprinkles for topping (optional but encouraged)

MOLTEN CHOCOLATE–RED VELVET CAKES WITH CREAM CHEESE ICE CREAM

Here we combine two of the most popular dessert trends of the 1990s into one fantastic plant-based treat. Did you know that chocolate lava cake was considered the pinnacle of French fine-dining desserts until it fell from grace onto the dessert menus of chain restaurants like Chili's and Domino's? And did you know that the red armadillo cake in the movie *Steel Magnolias* (1989) kicked off a decade of red velvet madness in the United States? These are just two fun facts to mull over while you make this delicious chocolate beet cake with an oozing center and cream cheese ice cream.

THE PLAN: Chill the can of coconut cream overnight and freeze the banana. Make the ice cream. Roast and process the beets. Make the cake batter and bake the cake. While the cake is baking, remove the ice cream from the freezer to allow it to loosen a bit.

To make the ice cream, chill the can of coconut cream in the refrigerator overnight. (We now have the habit of keeping a can in the fridge so that it's ready when we need it.) The next day, remove the can from the refrigerator. Do not shake it before opening it, as you want the liquid at the bottom to remain separate from the solids. Open the can and spoon ½ cup of the hardened coconut cream from the top into a high-speed blender. Alternatively, a bowl and an electric mixer can be used. (Reserve the balance of the can's contents for smoothies.)

If using the guar gum and xanthan gum, combine them along with the maple syrup in a small microwave-safe bowl and whisk together until fully emulsified. Microwave the mixture for 10 seconds, then whisk again and let cool to room temperature before using.

Add the frozen banana, cream cheese, salt, and the cooled maple syrup mixture, if using, or the maple syrup to the coconut cream. Begin blending or beating on low speed and gradually move to high speed, stopping to scrape down the sides as you go. Continue to blend until the mixture is smooth and creamy.

Transfer the mixture to an airtight container and freeze until you have a scoop-friendly ice cream, at least 4–6 hours or up to overnight. It will become very hard, so you'll need to let it rest outside the freezer for 30 minutes before scooping. (Yes, this ice cream is way more high maintenance than regular ice cream.)

To make the cakes, preheat the oven to 375°F. Drizzle the beets with a little olive oil, wrap each beet individually in aluminum foil, and place on a small sheet pan. Roast until a sharp knife pierces easily to the center of a beet, about 1 hour. Remove from the oven, unwrap, and let cool. To skin each beet, wrap it in a paper towel and give it a gentle squeeze. The skin will slide off.

Transfer the beets to a food processor and pulse until smooth. If the beets still have a little texture, it is good for the texture of the cakes. Measure 1 cup of the processed beets for the cakes. Reserve the remainder for another use.

FOR THE ICE CREAM

1 can (14 oz) Aroy-D full-fat coconut cream

¼ teaspoon guar gum (optional)

⅛ teaspoon xanthan gum (optional)

2 tablespoons pure maple syrup

1 banana, peeled, cut into ½-inch chunks, and frozen

½ cup Miyoko's cream cheese

¼ teaspoon salt

FOR THE CAKES

1 lb red beets, trimmed

Olive oil for drizzling

Nonstick cooking spray or Miyoko's unsalted butter for the pan

½ cup high-quality unsweetened cocoa powder or cacao powder, plus more for the pan

1 cup unsweetened almond milk

2 teaspoons fresh lemon juice

½ cup plus 2 tablespoons organic sugar

¼ cup coconut oil, melted and cooled

1 teaspoon pure vanilla extract

1 cup all-purpose flour or gluten-free flour of choice

1 teaspoon baking powder

¼ teaspoon kosher salt

½ cup semisweet chocolate chips, melted and cooled

4 oz high-quality dark chocolate, such as Valrhona brand, broken into 8 equal squares

Spray 8 standard muffin-pan wells with cooking spray or grease with butter. Then dust the wells with cocoa powder and tap out the excess.

In a large bowl, mix together the almond milk and lemon juice. Add the sugar, coconut oil, vanilla, and beet purée and beat with a whisk until foamy. Then add the cocoa powder, flour, baking powder, and salt and mix well. Add the melted chocolate and mix until fully incorporated.

Spoon enough batter into each prepared muffin well to fill it two-thirds full. Push a square of the dark chocolate down into the center of each cake. Top each well with an additional spoonful of batter.

Place the cakes in the oven. At the same time, remove the ice cream from the freezer so it can loosen up a bit. Bake the cakes until their edges have pulled away slightly from the pan sides and the tops no longer appear wet, 10-15 minutes.

Remove the muffin pan from the oven and let the cakes cool in the pan on a wire rack for 5 minutes. Then, using a butter knife, gently loosen each cake from the pan sides. Invert a large plate on top of the pan, flip the pan and plate over together, and lift off the pan. The cakes should pop right out.

Place each cake on a dessert plate. Garnish each cake with a pinch of Maldon salt and a dusting of cocoa powder, if using, and set a scoop of the ice cream alongside.

Maldon sea salt for garnish

High-quality unsweetened cocoa powder or cacao powder for garnish (optional)

NOTE: To save time, look for cooked beets in the produce section of the market. Vacuum-packed Love brand organic cooked beets are a good choice.

BUCKWHEAT BLUEBERRY TRES LECHES JAR CAKES WITH COCONUT WHIPPED CREAM

This combination of blueberries, moist, coconutty cake, and fluffy cream makes for an incredibly addictive bite. And because the overall dessert is much lighter than traditional *tres leches* cake, you're probably going to want a lot of bites. All this said, I'm not sure you can call these jar cakes "healthy." But they are perfect if, like us, you have trouble being a one-bite dessert person. And if you don't want to use blueberries, I've made this dish with strawberries, peaches, mango, and even bananas, and all were awesome.

THE PLAN: Put the can of coconut cream or coconut milk for the whipped coconut cream in the refrigerator overnight. Make the cakes. While they cool, whip the cream, make the fortified milk, and cook the compote. Assemble the dessert and serve.

Refrigerate the can of coconut cream or milk for the coconut whipped cream overnight. Put a bowl in the refrigerator at the same time.

The next day, make the cakes. Preheat the oven to 350°F. Spray a 6-well standard muffin pan with cooking spray.

In a bowl, stir together the almond milk, oil, vinegar, vanilla bean paste, and almond extract, if using, mixing well. Let rest for 5 minutes. In a second bowl, stir together the all-purpose and buckwheat flours, baking powder, baking soda, sugar, and salt, mixing well. Add the liquid ingredients to the dry ingredients and stir just until well mixed.

Transfer the batter to the prepared muffin pan, filling each well one-third full. Bake until a toothpick inserted into the center of a cake comes out clean, 20–25 minutes. Remove from the oven, immediately turn the cakes out onto a wire rack, turn them upright, and let cool completely.

Make the coconut whipped cream as directed, reserving any liquid from the can for the fortified milk. Refrigerate the whipped cream until serving.

To make the fortified milk, in a blender, combine all the ingredients and blend until smooth. Set aside.

To make the compote, in a saucepan, combine the blueberries, sugar, lemon juice, salt, and cinnamon over medium heat and cook, stirring a bit to combine and prevent sticking, for 2 minutes. In a small bowl, stir together the cornstarch and water and immediately add to the pan. Continue to cook, stirring often, until the mixture comes to a boil, 1–2 minutes. Immediately remove from the heat and let cool to room temperature.

To assemble the cakes, line up six 4-oz widemouthed Mason jars or similar vessels. Place a cake on the bottom of each jar. Then, using a fork, poke deep holes into each cake. Pour the fortified milk over the cakes, dividing it evenly, and then let the cakes rest for 15 minutes to soak up the liquid. Top each cake with the whipped cream and finish with a few spoonfuls of compote. Chill for 1 hour before serving. The cakes, minus the compote, can be assembled up to a day in advance and the compote added just before serving.

NOTE: If you want to make this super-duper easy, substitute muffins made from Just Egg and Against the Grain Gourmet's gluten-free yellow cake mix. Just be sure the granulated sugar is organic, as most white sugar in the United States contains bovine bone char to aid in whitening.

Coconut Whipped Cream (page 142)

FOR THE CAKES
Nonstick cooking spray
¾ cup unsweetened almond milk
2 tablespoons extra-virgin olive oil
½ teaspoon distilled white vinegar
1 teaspoon vanilla bean paste (preferred) or pure vanilla extract
½ teaspoon pure almond extract (optional)
1 cup all-purpose flour
2 tablespoons buckwheat flour
1 teaspoon baking powder
1 teaspoon baking soda
⅔ cup organic granulated sugar
¼ teaspoon kosher salt

FOR THE FORTIFIED MILK
1 can (14 oz) Aroy-D full-fat coconut milk
Liquid reserved from coconut cream or milk
2 tablespoons organic granulated sugar
½ teaspoon kosher salt
1 teaspoon pure vanilla extract
1 cup cashews, toasted (see Note, page 33)

FOR THE COMPOTE
1 cup fresh or frozen blueberries
1 tablespoon coconut sugar (preferred) or organic granulated sugar
½ teaspoon fresh lemon juice
Pinch of kosher salt
Pinch of freshly grated (preferred) or ground cinnamon
¼ teaspoon cornstarch
2 tablespoons water

GRILLED PEACHES & ICE CREAM

Blair is obsessed with peaches because he grew up in Georgia, where folks are so crazy about peaches that the fruit is even on the state's license plates. Thus, every San Francisco "summer" (aka our first hot week in September), I find Blair on our porch grilling peaches in his board shorts with a Corona tallboy in his hand.

If you've never tried a grilled peach, you should really get on it. Just make sure the peach is ripe enough to be sweet but not so soft that it falls apart on the grill. This recipe is just one of many variations on a grilled-peach dessert theme we play around with all summer long. It goes like this: Grill peaches. Serve them warm with a cold nondairy dessert product (here, plant-based ice cream). Drizzle with sauce (here, honey or caramel). For more ideas, see the Note below right.

THE PLAN: If you are using the hazelnuts, preheat the oven. Next, start the grill. While the grill is heating, make the vanilla salt and the honey or caramel sauce and toast the nuts. Grill the peaches, assemble each serving, and serve.

If using the hazelnuts, preheat the oven to 350°F. While the oven is heating, prepare the grill for direct cooking over medium-high heat.

Put the salt into a small bowl. Using a sharp knife, split the vanilla bean lengthwise and, using the tip of the knife, scrape out the seeds (they look like black tar) into the bowl with the salt. Using your fingertips, mix the vanilla seeds into the salt, dispersing them evenly. You will have more vanilla salt than you need for this recipe. The remainder will keep in an airtight container at room temperature for up to 1 year.

Now, choose between the honey and the caramel sauce. If you opt for the honey and do not have it on hand, make it. If you opt for the caramel sauce, select a heavy saucepan and clean it well by wiping it with a wet paper towel and a little vinegar to remove any bits of debris, which can cause caramel to crystallize. Then add the sugar to the pan and shake the pan gently to spread the sugar in an even layer. Place over medium-low heat and heat without stirring until the sugar melts and turns a medium amber, about 10 minutes. You'll need to watch the progress and turn the heat down if it starts to burn.

Slowly add the vinegar. The liquid will splatter and bubble a bit, so be careful. (Try not to inhale the vapor from the boiling vinegar. It's not a pleasant experience.) Cook, gently swirling the pan from time to time, until the vinegar and caramel come together in a uniform liquid, then continue to cook, stirring occasionally, until the sauce coats the back of a spoon, 3–5 minutes. Whisk in the butter, a tablespoon at a time, whisking after each addition until fully incorporated before adding the next. Then remove the pan from the heat and keep warm. You need only ½ cup of the sauce. The leftover sauce will keep in an airtight container in the refrigerator for up to 1 month.

If using the hazelnuts, spread them on a sheet pan and toast in the oven until they are fragrant and have taken on color, about 20 minutes. Let cool, then roughly chop or crush with a rolling pin and set aside.

2 tablespoons kosher salt

1 vanilla bean

½ cup Clover Blossom Honey (page 153), warmed (optional)

FOR THE CARAMEL SAUCE (OPTIONAL)

1 cup cider vinegar, plus more for cleaning the pan

1 cup organic sugar

4 tablespoons Miyoko's unsalted butter

¼ cup hazelnuts (optional)

4 ripe but firm peaches

Olive oil for brushing

4 scoops nondairy cinnamon ice cream

NOTE: Here are some additional ideas for dressing up this versatile dessert. Use whatever flavor of nondairy ice cream jumps out at you, or try Kite Hill ricotta cheese in place of the ice cream. You can also serve the whole thing atop a thin piece of corn bread (grilled if you like). And for a finishing herbal touch, add a sprinkle of fresh mint, basil, or lemon balm.

Halve and pit the peaches. Brush the entire exterior of each peach half with oil. Grill the peaches directly over the fire, turning once, until golden brown and just cooked through, about 2 minutes on each side.

To assemble, place 2 peach halves, cut side up, on each dessert plate. Top with the ice cream, season with a little vanilla salt, and sprinkle with the nuts (if using). Drizzle with the warm caramel sauce or honey and serve.

ON DESSERT SALT: Dessert salt is a culinary concept that should be more widespread. Many desserts are greatly improved by a finishing sprinkle of salt. In the case of the grilled peaches, we up the ante by mixing the salt with vanilla seeds. It's a simple thing, but it has high impact. You'll have more vanilla salt than you'll need for the peaches, so experiment with sprinkling it on other desserts, like the cheesecake on (page 138).

COCONUT CHIA PUDDING WITH MANGO ICE CREAM & FRESH PINEAPPLE

If you like piña coladas—and you have half a brain—you will probably like this dessert. Refreshing, impressive, and vaguely reminiscent of a tropical cocktail, it's an easy win.

 THE PLAN: Make and chill the chia pudding. Prepare all the garnishes, then assemble and serve.

To make the pudding, in a bowl, whisk together the chia seeds, maple syrup, vanilla bean paste, salt, and ¾ cup of the coconut milk. Let stand until you see the seeds begin to rehydrate, about 5 minutes. Then whisk again, breaking up any lumps. Now whisk in the remaining ¾ cup coconut milk, cover, and refrigerate for at least 6 hours or up to 24 hours. (Adding the coconut milk in two batches makes the milk easier to incorporate and helps prevent lumping.)

Remove the pudding from the refrigerator. If it is too thick, whisk in a little more coconut milk. If it's too thin, add more chia seeds, whisking in a small amount at a time and waiting for 5 minutes until they hydrate before adding more.

When you are satisfied with its consistency, divide the pudding evenly among individual serving bowls, spooning it into the bottom. Top each serving with a scoop of ice cream, placing it in the center. Then fan the pineapple and mango pieces out around the ice cream to resemble rays of the sun. Sprinkle the pomegranate seeds, mint, and coconut in little piles around each bowl and serve.

FOR THE PUDDING

½ cup chia seeds

2 tablespoons pure maple syrup

1 teaspoon vanilla bean paste, or seeds from 1 vanilla bean

¼ teaspoon kosher salt

1½ cups Aroy-D full-fat coconut milk, plus more if needed

FOR SERVING

4 scoops mango, coconut, or other tropical-flavored ice cream

⅓ cup thinly sliced pineapple

½ cup diced mango, in ½-inch dice

¼ cup pomegranate seeds

¼ cup loosely packed mint leaves, torn

¼ cup unsweetened shredded dried coconut, toasted

LEMON SHORTCAKE ICE POPS WITH CARDAMOM & PISTACHIO

One of Blair's favorite ice-cream truck treats as a child was a strawberry shortcake bar, and it is easy to understand why. The combination of artificial fruit flavor, "cream," and cake crumble is tough to beat.

This recipe is Blair's attempt to turn that Good Humor shortcake memory into a more grown-up dessert. He blends the oh-so-sophisticated combination of cardamom and lemon into a coconut-milk ice pop and then rolls it in pistachios, rose petals, and lemon cookie crumbs before serving. Although the guar gum and xanthan gum are optional, adding them yields a better consistency.

 THE PLAN: Make the ice pops mixture and freeze. Then make the coating. Let the ice pops thaw briefly before rolling them in the coating.

To make the ice pops, in a blender, combine all the ingredients and blend on medium speed until smooth. Divide the mixture evenly among six ice pop molds, insert the sticks, and freeze until frozen solid, 4–6 hours.

To make the coating, toast the pistachios as directed in the Note on page 33. Let cool, transfer to a food processor, and pulse until reduced to crumb-like bits. Transfer to a small, shallow bowl.

Break up the cookies, add to the processor, and pulse until reduced to small crumbs. Measure ¾ cup crumbs and add to the pistachios.

Add the salt to the bowl with the nuts and cookie crumbs, pour the butter on top, and, using your fingers, mix together everything until you have a soft crumb mixture. If using, add the rose petals, gently crumbling them with your fingers into the bowl. Mix well and set aside.

When the ice pops are ready, line a sheet pan or large plate with waxed paper. Run the molds under warm water briefly, then remove the ice pops from the molds and place them on the prepared pan. Let thaw for 2–3 minutes so the crumb topping will stick.

One at a time, place the ice pops in the coating mixture. Using a spoon or your hands, scoop the mixture over the ice pop, coating evenly and pressing gently so the mixture adheres. As the ice pops are coated, return them to the pan, and then return the pan with all the ice pops to the freezer for 15 minutes to set the coating. Wrap each ice pop in plastic wrap and return them to the freezer until ready to serve. They are best eaten within 1 week of being made, but they will keep much longer.

FOR THE ICE POPS

1 can (14 oz) Aroy-D full-fat coconut milk

¼ cup pure maple syrup

1 tablespoon grated lemon zest

1 teaspoon vanilla bean paste

½ teaspoon freshly ground cardamom

¼ teaspoon Himalayan black or kosher salt

¼ teaspoon guar gum (optional)

⅛ teaspoon xanthan gum (optional)

FOR THE COATING

½ cup pistachios

Lucy's Lemon Goodness gluten-free cookies or other plant-based cookies, as needed to make ¾ cup crumbs

⅛ teaspoon kosher salt

1 tablespoon Miyoko's unsalted butter, melted

¼ cup food-grade dried rose petals or buds (optional)

S'MORE BROWNIE CUPCAKES WITH BRÛLÉED MARSHMALLOW

Here, we bake a chocolate brownie with a graham cracker crust in a Mason jar and then top it with brûléed marshmallow fluff. It's a tad less messy than traditional s'mores and rather easy to make. If you are a strict plant-based eater, you may already know that Nabisco, Keebler, and Annie's all make honey-free graham crackers and that Trader Joe's and Dandies make vegan marshmallows.

Blair really hit his stride with this recipe when James was a newborn. I'm here to tell you that babies and blow torches can coexist peacefully. If you're not a fan of blow torches, you can also use your broiler to brown the marshmallow fluff.

THE PLAN: Prepare the cupcake batter and graham cracker crust and layer them in the Mason jars. While the cupcakes bake and cool, prepare the marshmallow fluff. Pipe the fluff onto the cupcakes, then torch and serve.

To make the cupcakes, preheat the oven to 350°F. Spray eight 4-oz widemouthed Mason jars with cooking spray.

In a large bowl, whisk together the flour, cocoa powder, granulated and coconut sugars, egg replacer, baking powder, and salt, mixing well. Add the almond milk, butter, and vanilla and stir until fully and evenly incorporated. Fold in ½ cup of the chocolate chips, distributing them evenly.

To make the crust, break up the graham crackers, drop them into a food processor, and pulse until evenly ground. Measure the crumbs and return 1 cup to the processor. (Snack on the rest.) Add the butter and pulse until the crumbs are evenly moistened. Spoon the crust mixture into the prepared jars, using a generous 1½ tablespoons for each jar. Using the back of a spoon (or something round that fits perfectly in the jar), firmly press against the mixture until it lies flat on the bottom of the jar.

Using a ¼-cup measuring scoop, pour the brownie batter over the graham cracker crust in each jar, distributing it evenly and covering the crust completely.

Arrange the jars on a sheet pan and place in the oven. Bake the cupcakes until the edges appear firm, about 45 minutes. Transfer the pan to a wire rack and immediately add the remaining chocolate chips, sprinkling them evenly on top. Let the cupcakes cool on the pan on a wire rack for about 30 minutes.

While the cupcakes cool, make the marshmallow fluff. In a bowl, using an electric mixer, whip together the chickpea liquid, powdered sugar, vanilla, and cream of tartar on high speed until stiff peaks form (they should stand on their own when the beater is lifted), 8–12 minutes. Add the granulated sugar and continue to whip until the peaks are both stiff and glossy, about 3 minutes longer. You should have 2 cups.

Continued on page 136...

FOR THE CUPCAKE BATTER

Nonstick cooking spray

⅔ cup almond flour

½ cup Dutch-process unsweetened cocoa powder, preferably Valrhona or Guittard brand

⅓ cup organic granulated sugar

⅓ cup coconut sugar

2 tablespoons Bob's Red Mill egg replacer, in powder form

1 teaspoon baking powder

½ teaspoon kosher salt

½ cup plus 2 tablespoons unsweetened almond milk

4 tablespoons Miyoko's unsalted butter, melted and cooled

1½ teaspoons pure vanilla extract

¾ cup dark chocolate chips (the larger the better)

FOR THE CRUST

1 box (8 oz) plant-based graham cracker squares

2 tablespoons Miyoko's unsalted butter, melted

FOR THE MARSHMALLOW FLUFF

6 tablespoons liquid from canned low-sodium chickpeas (aka aquafaba; see page 169)

3 tablespoons organic powdered sugar

1 teaspoon pure vanilla extract or vanilla bean paste

½ teaspoon cream of tartar

½ cup organic granulated sugar

Maldon sea salt, plain or smoked, for finishing

Spoon a dollop of the marshmallow fluff on top of each cupcake, distributing it evenly. Alternatively, spoon the marshmallow fluff into a pastry bag fitted with a ¾-inch round tip or into a resealable plastic bag and twist the top closed. If using a plastic bag, cut a 1-inch hole in a bottom corner. Then, applying gentle pressure at the top of the bag, pipe the fluff in the shape of a Hershey's Kiss on top of each cupcake.

To brown the marshmallow fluff with a blow torch, hold the ignited torch just above the fluff and allow the fluff to brown slowly. To brown the marshmallow fluff in a broiler, pre-heat the broiler and place the jars under the broiler until the fluff begins to turn golden brown, 2–4 minutes.

Finish each cupcake with a pinch of Maldon salt and serve. These cupcakes are best when eaten right away. The marshmallow topping will droop in time, so try to consume them within 2 days.

NOTE: These cupcakes can also be made in a standard muffin pan.

CHOCOLATE CHIP–ALMOND
BUTTER OATMEAL COOKIES

I'll occasionally find a candy-bar wrapper next to Blair's side of the bed. James often requests an ice pop as soon as he wakes up in the morning. And I eat chocolate every damn day. Yes, our family has a sweet tooth. But more and more we are leaning toward desserts we can feel good about eating often. These cookies are low glycemic, protein rich, and don't last long around here.

 THE PLAN: Mix the ingredients. Rest the dough (see sidebar). Bake. Eat.

In a large bowl, beat together the almond butter, egg replacer, and vanilla until smooth. In a medium bowl, stir together the flour, oats, sugar, and baking soda, mixing well. Add the dry ingredients to the wet ingredients and beat until smooth. (You can make this dough by hand using a wooden spoon or on medium speed with a stand mixer fitted with the paddle attachment or an electric mixer.) Add the nuts and chocolate chips and stir until evenly distributed. Now this is the hard part: let the dough rest for at least 2 hours to allow the oats and flour to hydrate (see sidebar).

Preheat the oven to 375°F. Line a sheet pan with parchment paper.

Using a 1-oz cookie scoop or a 1-tablespoon measure, shape the dough into 2-tablespoon-size balls and arrange them on the prepared pan, spacing them about 2 inches apart. (You can also use parchment paper to shape the dough into a log about 2 inches in diameter and then cut the log into 20 uniform slices.)

Bake the cookies until the edges turn golden brown, 10–15 minutes. Transfer the pan to a wire rack and immediately garnish each cookie with a pinch of salt. Let cool on the pan for 10 minutes, then transfer the cookies to the rack to cool completely. You know what to do from here.

1 cup creamy almond butter

2 tablespoons Bob's Red Mill Egg Replacer, prepared for 2 whole eggs according to package directions

1 tablespoon pure vanilla extract

½ cup almond or all-purpose flour

½ cup Bob's Red Mill quick-cooking steel-cut oats

¾ cup coconut sugar

1 teaspoon baking soda

½ cup chopped walnuts or pecans

½ cup dark chocolate chips

Maldon sea salt for garnish

RESTING COOKIE DOUGH: It seems ridiculous, right? The outrage! I don't want to wait to eat my cookies any longer than I have to. Well, let's allow Blair to step onto the soapbox for a moment. The longer the dough rests—and that can be as long as 10 days (horrors!)—the more evenly the flour and oats will bake, making a taste test-approved superior cookie every time. For these oatmeal cookies, we recommend allowing the dough to rest for at least 2 hours. And if you decide to substitute all-purpose flour or another flour in the recipe, the dough should rest for at least 6 hours so the flour can properly hydrate. Now, if you want a wider, flatter cookie, it's fine not to chill the dough as it rests. But if you prefer a slightly plumper cookie, slip the dough into the refrigerator to rest.

MEYER LEMON CHEESECAKE
WITH SEASONAL FRUIT

Whenever Blair cut the sugar content of Wildseed's desserts, the restaurant would receive more compliments and sales would go up. This leads us to the natural conclusion that people prefer their desserts less sweet these days. This Meyer lemon cheesecake follows the trend. It's lower in sugar than your typical cheesecake, which allows some of the more subtle flavors of vanilla, basil, and ripe fruit to shine through. For this tangy, lemony dessert, we recommend using the ripest seasonal fruit you can find. Its sweetness will create the perfect contrast with the zingy lemon flavor.

THE PLAN: Make and bake the crust. Make the filling, pour it onto the crust, bake the cheesecake, and then chill. Prepare the fruit topping and allow to macerate, then plate and serve.

To make the crust, preheat the oven to 350°F. Line the bottom of an 8- or 9-inch springform pan with parchment paper.

Break up the graham crackers and drop them into a food processor. Add the brown sugar and salt and pulse until the crackers are ground to fine crumbs. Measure the crumbs and return 1½ cups to the processor. (Snack on the rest.) Add the butter, a little at a time, and pulse until the crumbs are evenly moistened. Turn the crumb mixture into the prepared pan and press firmly and evenly against the bottom of the pan.

Partially bake the crust until set, about 8 minutes. Let cool in the pan on a wire rack.

To make the filling, wipe out the food processor. Add the cream cheese, whipped cream, granulated sugar, maple syrup, vanilla, salt, and cornstarch and process until smooth and creamy, about 1 minute. Add the agar powder and lemon zest and process until well mixed.

Pour the filling onto the cooled crust. Smooth the top with an offset spatula and then gently lift and tap the pan on a work surface to settle the cake and further smooth the top. Bake until lightly browned on top, about 1 hour. Let cool completely in the pan on a wire rack. Cover and refrigerate for at least 1 hour or up to overnight before serving.

While the cheesecake is chilling, prepare the fruit. In a bowl, combine the fruit, oil, honey to taste, basil, and salt and stir gently. Allow the fruit to macerate until the cake is chilled.

To serve, remove the cake from the refrigerator. Hold the blade of a sharp chef's knife under hot water for 10 seconds, then wipe it dry. Unclasp the pan sides and lift them off. If there is sticking, run the knife or an offset spatula around the edge to loosen the sides. Wet the knife again, wipe it dry, and cut a slice from the cake while the blade is hot. Transfer the slice to a dessert plate. Repeat, heating and drying the knife each time, until all the slices are cut and on plates. Gently spoon some fruit on top of each slice and serve.

FOR THE CRUST

1 box (8 oz) plant-based graham cracker squares

1 tablespoon firmly packed brown sugar

¼ teaspoon kosher salt

½ cup Miyoko's unsalted butter, melted and cooled

FOR THE FILLING

2 lb Miyoko's cream cheese

¾ cup coconut whipped cream, homemade (page 142) or store-bought

⅔ cup organic granulated sugar

¼ cup pure maple syrup

1 tablespoon vanilla bean paste

Pinch of kosher salt

¼ cup cornstarch or arrowroot

1 tablespoon agar powder

2 teaspoons grated Meyer lemon zest, or 1 teaspoon each grated regular lemon zest and tangerine zest

FOR THE FRUIT

2 cups cut-up ripe seasonal fruit, in ½-inch pieces (such as pineapple, kiwifruit, or pear in the winter and nectarine, peach, or strawberry in the summer)

2 tablespoons extra-virgin olive oil

1–2 tablespoons Clover Blossom Honey (page 153)

1 tablespoon fresh basil or tarragon leaves, torn into small pieces

Pinch of kosher salt

Drinks

CAROLYN'S HOT CACAO

This treat is the purest, most delicious form of hot chocolate. The ultimate proof? Three-year-old James loves it just as much as we do. Cacao powder, which is made from unroasted cacao beans, is less processed than cocoa powder and contains high amounts of selenium and magnesium. Maca root is loaded with vitamin C, plus copper, iron, potassium, and more—not to mention it boosts your libido and your mood. All of this is to say, this recipe yields legitimately great-for-you hot chocolate. But even if you don't care about all of the benefits, you'll love the way this tastes. Promise.

In a small saucepan, combine the cacao powder, maca powder, and ¼ cup of the water over medium-high heat and stir to dissolve the powders into a slurry. Add the almond milk, honey, coconut oil, salt, and cinnamon and heat, continuing to stir, until all the ingredients are incorporated and the mixture is piping hot.

Divide the hot cacao between two mugs and serve immediately with a dollop of coconut whipped cream, if desired.

COCONUT WHIPPED CREAM: This is a light, fluffy, delicious dairy-free whipped cream substitute that's a total breeze to make. Refrigerate 1 can (14 oz) coconut cream or full-fat coconut milk in the coldest part of your refrigerator overnight. (We almost always have a can lurking in the back of our fridge waiting for a chilly hot cacao day.) We recommend Savoy coconut cream or Aroy-D full-fat coconut milk. Nature's Charm markets a "coconut whipping cream" that has some added sugar, and you use the whole can, not just the solids. Put a mixing bowl or a stand mixer bowl into the fridge to chill at the same time.

The next day, remove the coconut cream or milk and the bowl from the refrigerator. Do not shake the can before opening it, as you want any liquid at the bottom to remain separate from the solids. Open the can and spoon off the thick cream on top into the chilled bowl. Reserve any liquid in the can. Using a handheld mixer or a stand mixer fitted with the whisk attachment, beat the coconut cream on high speed until soft peaks form, about 30 seconds. If it's too chunky, add some of the reserved liquid to smooth it out. Add ¼ cup organic powdered sugar, sifted, and ½ teaspoon pure vanilla extract and continue to beat until stiff peaks form, about 1 minute. Cover and refrigerate until needed. It will keep for up to 1 week.

If you don't have time to make the coconut whipped cream, look for dairy-free So Delicious Cocowhip (or a similar product) in your supermarket's freezer section. It's pretty darn good in a pinch.

2 tablespoons cacao powder, preferably Nativas brand

2 teaspoons maca powder, preferably Nativas brand

1 cup water

1 ½ cups unsweetened almond milk (see Note)

2 tablespoons Clover Blossom Honey (page 153)

1 teaspoon coconut oil

Healthy pinch of sea salt

Few shakes of ground cinnamon

Coconut whipped cream, homemade (see Note) or store-bought (optional)

NOTE: Califa sweetened vanilla almond milk is great in this recipe.

HOT LEMON-CAYENNE-HONEY TISANE

If you start to feel an illness coming on, drink this immediately. Or drink it often to shorten the course of a cold that's already settled in. This recipe packs many different immune boosters into one glass and tastes calming and clearing when your sinuses and throat are aching for some love and attention. It's incredibly effective, and we find ourselves recommending it to friends all the time. Immunity is a major topic of conversation these days, so we figured we'd pass it along.

In a saucepan, combine the garlic, ginger, and cayenne. Halve the lemons, squeeze the juice into the pan, then throw in the spent peels. Add the water and bring to a boil over high heat. Remove from the heat and stir in the honey and the thyme, if using. Cover and let steep for 10 minutes.

Pour the mixture through a fine-mesh sieve into a pitcher. (I sometimes skip this step when I am very sick and lazy.) Stir in the elderberry syrup and echinacea.

Divide evenly between two glasses and sip slowly so you feel all the benefits setting in.

NOTE: Thyme dramatically alters the flavor of this drink but is fabulous for immunity. If you don't like the flavor, leave it out.

4 cloves garlic, minced

2-inch piece fresh ginger, minced

2 teaspoons cayenne pepper

2 lemons

4 cups water

3 tablespoons Clover Blossom Honey (page 153) or agave nectar

2 tablespoons fresh thyme leaves (see Note), optional

½ teaspoon elderberry syrup

½ teaspoon liquid echinacea

GREEN CHILE-INFUSED VODKA
WITH CUCUMBER SHRUB

Did you know that you can gauge the heat of a chile simply by looking at it? Here's the trick: the smaller the pepper, the higher its rating on the Scoville scale, which is used to measure a chile's pungency.

Now about this cocktail: We love it because it combines cooling and spicy sensations in one sip. Here, you will also learn how to make spicy vodka, which will greatly improve your Bloody Mary game and thus your social life—and thus your overall life. Who knew chiles could do so much for you?

To make the vodka, quarter all the fresh chiles. The seeds carry much of the heat, so discard or keep them depending on how spicy you want the vodka to be. Then combine the fresh chiles, the chipotle chiles, ginger, and vodka in a large Mason jar or similar widemouthed container with a lid. Cap tightly and shake it a few times to mix well. Let the mixture sit at room temperature for at least 3 days or up to 1 week. The longer it sits, the more powerful the flavor.

Line a fine-mesh sieve with cheesecloth and strain the vodka through the sieve. Using a funnel, return the vodka to its original bottle and cap tightly. Store in a cool, dry cupboard.

To make the simple syrup, in a small saucepan, combine the water and sugar and bring to a simmer over medium heat, stirring to dissolve the sugar. Remove from the heat, let cool, transfer to an airtight container, and refrigerate. It will keep for up to 1 month.

To make the cocktail, in a blender or food processer, combine the cucumber, lemon juice, and simple syrup and process until a juice forms. Line a fine-mesh sieve with cheesecloth and strain the juice through the sieve.

Fill a cocktail shaker a little more than half full with ice. Add the cucumber juice and vodka, cover, and shake vigorously. Strain into two tumblers filled with ice. Top with the club soda, dividing evenly. Stir gently and serve.

NOTE: We like FAIR. quinoa vodka not only because it tastes good but also because it is produced by a fair trade-certified company committed to stringent economic, environmental, and social standards. Feel free to use your favorite brand.

FOR THE SPICY VODKA

16 fresh chiles of differing size and heat, such as 4 each jalapeño, serrano, red Thai, and habanero or cayenne

3 tablespoons dried chipotle chiles or red pepper flakes

2-inch piece fresh ginger, cut into 4 pieces

1 bottle (700 ml) FAIR. quinoa vodka (see Note)

FOR THE SIMPLE SYRUP

½ cup water

½ cup organic sugar

FOR THE COCKTAIL

1 large cucumber, about ½ lb, roughly chopped

Juice of 1 lemon

2 tablespoons simple syrup (above)

4 oz spicy vodka (above)

4 oz club soda

MAPLE-CINNAMON WHISKEY SOUR

This one's for all you frothy-cocktail lovers out there. There's a great trick for creating this froth, or fizz, without egg whites. You can use the liquid from a can of chickpeas—called aquafaba by bar nerds—to create an almost identical effect. All you have to do is shake this liquid up (vigorously) with your cocktail ingredients, and boom, you've got foam.

The maple-cinnamon combination in this drink goes especially well with bourbon, rye, or whiskey, but you can easily substitute mezcal (reposado or añejo would be especially good, dark rum, or even vodka if you are avoiding brown booze. Cheers.

Fill a cocktail shaker a little more than half full with ice. Add the whiskey, lemon juice, chickpea liquid, maple syrup, cinnamon, and the bitters, if using. Cover and shake vigorously for 1 minute.

Strain into two rocks glasses filled with ice. Garnish the foam with a drop or two of additional bitters for a dramatic flourish if you like.

2 oz whiskey, bourbon, rye, or aged mezcal

1 oz fresh lemon juice

1 oz liquid from canned low-sodium chickpeas (aquafaba, see page 169)

¾ oz pure maple syrup

Pinch of ground cinnamon (optional)

2 dashes of Angostura bitters or bitters of choice (optional)

SPICE & BUBBLES

Remember mocktails? Nonalcoholic cocktails have long been the red-headed stepchildren of drink menus—often both lacking nuance and loaded with sugar. But that's changing. Interesting nonalcoholic spirits from Seedlip, Kin, and others have hit the market. These base spirits are made from different root, spice, and fruit extracts and are meant to be mixed with other ingredients in cocktails. For example, the Seedlip Spice 94 in this recipe is steeped with allspice, cardamom, citrus peel, and barks of oak and cascarilla to mimic the tannic, spice-laden experience of gin. This particular cocktail also incorporates the potency of pure citrus, ginger, and cardamom bitters. The end result packs enough of a punch that you don't want to gulp it all down in one minute, just as you wouldn't a boozy cocktail.

Fill a cocktail shaker a little more than half full with ice. Add the Seedlip Spice 94, lime juice, bitters, and cinnamon syrup and shake vigorously. Strain into a cocktail glass and top off with the ginger beer. Garnish with the nutmeg and serve.

1 ½ oz Seedlip Spice 94

¾ oz fresh lime juice

½ oz Fee Brothers cardamom bitters

½ oz cinnamon syrup

3 oz ginger beer, chilled

Freshly grated nutmeg for garnish

SMOKY CARROT COCKTAIL

We took our first sip of a mezcal-carrot cocktail in St. Augustine, Florida, when we were visiting Blair's parents one Christmas. The smokiness of mezcal pairs magically with the sweet, vegetal notes in carrot. (To the bartender at Barley Republic Public House, if you are reading this, you rock.) As soon as we got home, we tried to re-create the drink while playing with different salts and sugars to stick to the rim of the glass. We love the combo we landed on, which we have detailed here. The orange color of this drink is also a showstopper.

To coat the rim, put the Tajín seasoning on a small plate. Slide the flesh part of the lime wedge around the rim of a tumbler to moisten it. Roll the rim of the glass in the seasoning to coat and set aside. Repeat with a second glass.

Fill a cocktail shaker a little more than half full with ice. Add the carrot juice, mezcal, chile liqueur, lime juice, and agave nectar and shake vigorously. Strain into the prepared glasses, then garnish each glass with a lime wedge and serve.

FOR THE RIM

2 tablespoons Tajín Clásico Seasoning

1 lime wedge

6 oz carrot juice

2 oz mezcal

2 oz Ancho Reyes ancho chile liqueur

2 oz fresh lime juice

1 oz agave nectar

2 lime wedges

Fixins
& Basics

MARINATED FETA WITH CHIMICHURRI

Since you don't have to cook chimichurri, it's one of the quickest and easiest ways to add major depth of flavor to a dish. It also keeps well in the fridge. Here, we marinate feta in chimichurri for a delicious appetizer, which we serve with grilled flatbread. We also like to sprinkle the chimichurri over grilled vegetables, salads, cooked beans, and Just Egg, or spread it on sandwiches, crackers, or toast.

 THE PLAN: Make the chimichurri in the blender. Cut the feta and toss with the chimichurri.

To make the chimichurri, in a blender, combine the parsley, cilantro, arugula, garlic, Aleppo pepper, salt, and oil and blend until evenly combined, stopping to scrape down the sides of the blender once or twice to ensure everything is blended evenly. If the ingredients become warm from friction, let them cool down for a bit before the next step. Add the vinegar and lemon zest and incorporate them with a quick pulse or two. (Adding the vinegar after processing the herbs keeps it from turning them brown.) You should have about 1 cup chimichurri. Use immediately, or transfer to an airtight container and refrigerate for up to 1 month.

To marinate the feta, put it into a bowl and spoon up to ½ cup chimichurri on top. Using a spoon, delicately toss them together, being careful to not break up the feta. Serve immediately, or store in an airtight container in the refrigerator for up to 1 month.

FOR THE CHIMICHURRI

½ cup packed fresh flat-leaf parsley leaves and some stems

½ cup roughly chopped cilantro with some stems

¼ cup packed arugula

1 clove garlic

¼ teaspoon Aleppo pepper, or ¼ teaspoon red pepper flakes

¼ teaspoon kosher salt

½ cup rice bran or vegetable oil

¼ cup red wine vinegar

Grated zest of ½ lemon

4–6 oz plant-based feta cheese, cut into ½-inch cubes

TOGARASHI

This classic Japanese spice blend includes citrus, seeds, ginger, chile, and seaweed. We use it on the beet poke in this book, and it's delicious over a wide range of things, from fresh fruit, raw or grilled vegetables, and rice or noodle dishes to popcorn and avocado toast. You can buy premade togarashi at the store, but there's a rather dramatic difference when you make it with fresh ingredients at home. Spices begin losing their potency after about a month, so we make our togarashi in a small batch to ensure it's always full of flavor.

THE PLAN: Preheat the oven, mix the ingredients, and dry them in the oven. Grind half of the dried mixture, then mix with the remaining half and the remaining ingredients and store.

Preheat the oven to 170°F or to the lowest setting possible. Line a small sheet pan with parchment paper.

In a small bowl, combine the chopped chiles, Sichuan peppercorn, tangerine and Meyer lemon zest, and ginger and mix well. Evenly spread the mixture on the prepared pan.

Place in the oven and leave to dry, stirring every 2 hours, for 6 hours (this step can also be done in a dehydrator).

Remove from the oven, let cool, then transfer half of the mixture to a spice grinder or high-speed blender and grind until the grains are about the size of kosher salt. (Make sure the blades are bone-dry so the ingredients don't stick to them.)

Return the ground mixture to the other half of the mixture, add the sesame seeds and nori, and mix well. Transfer to an airtight container and store at room temperature for up to 1 month.

2 tablespoons finely chopped whole dried chiles, such as árbol

1 tablespoon freshly ground Sichuan peppercorn

2 teaspoons grated tangerine zest

2 teaspoons grated Meyer lemon zest, or 2 ½ teaspoons grated tangerine zest and 1 ½ teaspoons grated regular lemon zest

2 teaspoons peeled and grated fresh ginger

1 tablespoon toasted sesame seeds

1 tablespoon finely chopped nori (about ½ sheet)

CLOVER BLOSSOM HONEY

This plant-based honey will make your head spin. It tastes just like high-quality bee honey. The recipe comes from Lauren Fitzgerald, the beverage director at Wildseed. She's been eating a plant-based diet for decades and can make one hell of a cocktail to boot. Orange blossom water and red clover blossoms are available at natural-food stores, vitamin stores, health-food shops, and online.

4 cups agave nectar

2 ½ tablespoons orange blossom water

2 tablespoons pure maple syrup

1 ½ tablespoons cider vinegar

½ vanilla bean

¼ cup dried red clover blossoms

 THE PLAN: Reduce the agave nectar and other ingredients on the stove top, then remove from the heat, add the red clover blossoms, steep, strain, and cool.

In a saucepan, combine the agave nectar, orange blossom water, maple syrup, vinegar, and vanilla bean and bring to a boil over medium-high heat. Immediately reduce the heat to low and simmer, stirring frequently, until reduced by one-third, about 10 minutes.

Remove from the heat, add the clover blossoms, and let steep for 10 minutes. Strain through a fine-mesh sieve and let cool. Store in an airtight container in the refrigerator for up to 1 month.

QUICK-PICKLED CARROTS

You—yes, you!—can make pickles in an hour. These are great as a stand-alone snack or as a condiment with almost any savory dish.

 THE PLAN: Peel the carrots and cut into ribbons. Make the pickling liquid. Combine and let stand for at least another 30 minutes before serving.

Trim and peel the carrots. Then, still using the peeler, slice the carrots lengthwise into long, thin ribbons.

In a bowl, combine the water, vinegar, agave nectar, and salt and stir to mix well and dissolve the salt. Submerge the carrot ribbons in the liquid and let stand at room temperature for at least 30 minutes before using. If you are short on time, use a microwave-safe bowl and microwave the carrots and liquid for 30 seconds, then let cool before using. They will keep in their liquid in an airtight container in the refrigerator for up to 3 months.

4 medium carrots

1 cup water

1 cup rice vinegar

¼ cup agave nectar

2 tablespoons kosher salt

PICKLED ONIONS

Onions are often an afterthought—so simple, so unassuming—but this recipe is one of the simplest ways to enhance almost every savory dish you prepare. Does your soup need a lift? Does your burger need a spark? Does your salad need a little star power? Add some pickled onions. Problem solved.

THE PLAN: Heat the brine on the stove top, immerse the onions in the hot brine, let cool, and eat!

Put the onions into a heatproof bowl. In a small saucepan, combine the vinegar, water, sugar, salt, and cinnamon (if using) and bring to a boil over high heat, stirring to dissolve the sugar. Remove from the heat and pour over the onions, making sure the onions are fully submerged. Let cool completely.

Use immediately, or store the onions in their liquid in an airtight container in the refrigerator for up to 3 months. The flavor improves with time.

2 cups thinly julienned red onions (about 2 small)

2 cups red wine vinegar

1 cup water

¼ cup organic sugar

1 tablespoon kosher salt

1 cinnamon stick (optional)

MINT-GARLIC WHITE SAUCE

The tang of lemony sour cream mixes with the freshness of mint, the heat of cayenne, and the depth of garlic to make a highly versatile, highly delicious sauce and dip. We especially like it with bread, fried balls of goodness (page 54), and grilled vegetables.

 THE PLAN: Whirl everything together in a food processor or blender. That's it!

In a food processor or blender, combine all the ingredients and process until smooth. Use immediately, or transfer to an airtight container and store in the refrigerator for up to 2 weeks.

½ cup Tofutti sour cream

¾ cup packed fresh mint leaves

1 clove garlic, smashed then minced

1 tablespoon water

1 tablespoon extra-virgin olive oil

1 teaspoon fresh lemon juice

½ teaspoon kosher salt

¼ teaspoon cayenne pepper

CUCUMBER YOGURT

This sauce and dip—our version of raita, the ubiquitous South Asian condiment—is a beautiful accompaniment to vegetables and adds an incomparable freshness to everything from soup to "meatballs." It's especially amazing when used to offset spicy dishes.

 THE PLAN: So easy—measure, mix, and serve.

In a bowl, combine all the ingredients and mix well. Use immediately, or store in an airtight container in the refrigerator for up to several days.

½ cup Tofutti sour cream

3 tablespoons za'atar

½ cup peeled, seeded, and diced cucumber

2 tablespoons fresh lemon juice

2 tablespoons grassy extra-virgin olive oil

Grated zest of ½ lemon

½ teaspoon kosher salt

COCONUT BACON

If you've never eaten coconut bacon, prepare to be amazed. It resembles the flavor and texture of shredded cooked bacon in an uncanny way. That said, you have to use the correct type of shredded coconut, which is typically labeled "coconut smiles" at grocery stores (because each piece has the shape of the smile part of a smiley face). "Smiles" or not, what you are looking for is dried coconut shavings, the bigger and thicker the better. SunRidge Farms is a reliable purveyor.

1 ½ cups unsweetened dried large coconut "smiles"

1 ½ tablespoons tamari or soy sauce

2 teaspoons liquid smoke

2 teaspoons pure maple syrup

1 ½ teaspoons smoked paprika

 THE PLAN: Combine all the ingredients. Bake, cool, and serve.

Preheat the oven to 350°F. Line a large sheet pan with parchment paper.

Put the coconut into a bowl, drizzle it with the tamari, liquid smoke, and maple syrup, sprinkle with the paprika, then mix well. Spread the coconut in an even layer on the prepared pan.

Bake the coconut, flipping it over halfway through baking, until the flakes are mostly dry and turning golden on the edges, 12–14 minutes. Keep an eye on the coconut as it bakes, as it can go from golden brown to burned fairly quickly. Let the coconut cool completely on the pan. It will crisp as it cools.

Use immediately, or transfer to an airtight container and store in the freezer for up to several months. There's no need to include time for thawing before using. It comes to room temperature in very little time.

NOTE: If the coconut softens over time, you can put it into an oven preheated to the lowest possible temperature or into a dehydrator to recrisp it. If using an oven, check on the coconut every 30 minutes or so to make sure it doesn't burn.

NACHO CHEESE

Did you know that the Food and Drug Administration won't allow Velveeta to label itself as "cheese"? Well this isn't cheese either, but you can feel good about eating it. To make it, you'll purée cashews with garlic, onion, roasted red peppers, and a medley of savory spices. Surprisingly, the color is quite similar to the color of Velveeta. That said, this dip has a different—dare we say, more complex—flavor profile. Both lovers and haters of Velveeta find it quite addictive.

 THE PLAN: Soak the cashews. Cook the onion and garlic in a sauté pan. Then blend together all the ingredients, cook, and serve.

Put the cashews into a bowl, add the ⅔ cup water, adding more if needed to immerse the nuts fully, and let soak at room temperature for at least 1 hour or up to 24 hours. The longer you soak them, the easier they are to process in the blender and the better the final texture. Drain the cashews and discard the water.

In a sauté pan, heat the oil over medium-high heat. Add the onion and garlic and cook, stirring occasionally, until the onion is translucent, about 8 minutes. Remove from the heat, transfer to a blender, and reserve the pan.

Add the cashews, peppers, lemon juice, nutritional yeast, paprika, salt, tapioca starch (if using), and garlic and onion powders to the blender and blend on high speed until smooth, 1-2 minutes.

Return the mixture to the pan, place over low heat, cover, and cook, stirring occasionally, until the flavors meld, about 20 minutes.

Serve immediately with vegetables or chips for dipping.

½ cup raw cashews

⅔ cup water, or as needed

1 teaspoon olive oil

1 tablespoon diced yellow onion

½ teaspoon chopped garlic (about 1 small clove)

¼ cup chopped roasted red peppers

Juice of ½ lemon (about 2 teaspoons)

2 tablespoons nutritional yeast

½ teaspoon smoked paprika

½ teaspoon kosher salt

½ teaspoon tapioca starch (optional)

¼ teaspoon garlic powder

¼ teaspoon onion powder

Vegetables or chips for serving

TRUFFLE BUTTER

Truffles are an especially fabulous addition to the plant-based diet, because they bring a flavor intensity that carnivores look for in meat. Depending on which truffle species you purchase—and there are many species—they can be earthy, gamy, oaky, nutty, or sweet. American and Asian truffles are easier on your wallet. European truffles are the most expensive and the most pungent. Some American truffles, such as pecan truffles, which grow in pecan orchards, are especially interesting. There are even some truffles being farmed in Northern California and northern New Zealand that rival the taste of their European cousins. Black truffles are typically considered stronger and earthier in flavor than the more delicate white truffles. In this recipe, be sure to match the color of your truffle with the color of your truffle oil. How do you use this delicious butter? Lately we've been putting it in pasta and mashed potatoes and on plant-based burgers.

½ lb Miyoko's unsalted butter, cut into 1-inch cubes

2 tablespoons white or black truffle pieces (no oil)

1 tablespoon white or black truffle oil

½ teaspoon truffle salt

 THE PLAN: Pulse together all the ingredients in a food processor or mix together by hand. Spoon onto plastic wrap, shape into a log, wrap, and refrigerate until well chilled.

You can make the butter in a food processor or in a bowl with a fork. To make the butter in a food processor, combine the butter, truffle pieces, truffle oil, and salt in the processor and pulse until the truffle pieces, oil, and salt are evenly mixed throughout the butter.

To make the butter in a bowl with a fork, have the butter at room temperature. Put the truffle pieces into a bowl and mash with a fork until reduced to a rough paste. Add the butter, truffle oil, and salt and continue to mash all the ingredients until a smooth butter forms.

Lay a large sheet of plastic wrap on a work surface. Spoon the butter onto the plastic wrap in a rough log shape. Then, with the aid of the plastic wrap, shape the butter into a uniform log about 1 inch in diameter. Wrap the log tightly in the plastic wrap and refrigerate until well chilled before using. It will keep in the refrigerator for up to 5 days or in the freezer for up to 1 month.

A GUIDE TO OTHER COMPOUND BUTTERS: Soften butter. Mix in such flavorful ingredients as herbs or spices. Then shape it into a log and chill. Congratulations, you've just made compound butter, which enhances almost anything you can think of that just came off the grill or out of the oven. The beauty of compound butter is that it makes quite an impact with a very low lift. The key is to slice the butter from the log as soon as your food exits the heat source so the hot food melts the butter on contact.

Here are some compound butters we make fairly often and how we use them.
- Honey cinnamon: Use on bread and biscuits, of course. Add a healthy dose of kosher salt and use it on corn or carrots, too.
- Lemon herb: Made with grated lemon zest, finely chopped fresh thyme and flat-leaf parsley, and minced garlic and shallot, this is a dream on grilled mushrooms and other vegetables.
- Red or yellow curry: Stir in curry paste. Use on roasted cauliflower. James goes nuts for it on rice.
- Chipotle lime: Work in diced canned chipotle chile and both the grated zest and the juice of lime. We like this on corn.
- Harissa butter: Mix in harissa paste. Delicious on carrots and sweet potatoes.
- Maple pecan: Work in finely diced pecans and pure maple syrup. Spread with abandon on waffles, toast, and muffins.

NO-FISH SAUCE

You'll be hard-pressed to achieve the right flavor profile in much of the Thai, Cambodian, and Vietnamese recipe canon without fish sauce, which packs a wallop of savory depth. The traditional product is made from fermented anchovies and salt. Blair developed a potent substitute that calls for dried mushrooms and seaweed and tamari.

THE PLAN: First, char the onion, then simmer it with the rest of the ingredients. Next, purée the mixture. Age the sauce in the refrigerator for at least 24 hours, then strain before using.

Cut the onion in half horizontally so the root and stem ends remain intact, then remove the outer peel from both halves. Turn on a burner on your stove top—gas or electric—to high. Place the onion halves cut side down directly on the burner and leave undisturbed until the underside is dark brown and charred, about 2 minutes. (Most Western cooks will find it unusual to cook vegetables directly on the burner, but it is quite common in Vietnamese cuisine.)

Transfer the onion halves to a 2-quart saucepan. Add the water, tamari, shiitake and porcini mushrooms, kombu, and stock base and bring to a boil over high heat. Cover, reduce the heat to a simmer, and simmer for 10 minutes.

Remove from the heat and let cool. Transfer the contents of the pan to a blender and blend until the vegetables are puréed as thoroughly as possible. Transfer to a container, cover loosely with plastic wrap, and allow to age in the refrigerator for at least 24 hours or up to 2 months.

Strain the sauce through a fine-mesh sieve into a container, pressing firmly on the solids to force out every drop of flavor. Transfer the strained sauce to an airtight container and store in the refrigerator for up to 1 month. Be sure always to give the container a shake before you use the sauce.

NOTE: Most Asian markets and well-stocked supermarkets carry a mushroom stock or broth base or seasoning, sometimes labeled "umami seasoning." Dark Horse umami bouillon or Better Than Bouillon mushroom base are good choices.

1 small white or yellow onion, unpeeled

2 cups water

1 cup tamari or soy sauce

1 cup dried shiitake mushrooms

½ cup dried porcini mushrooms

2 oz dried kombu seaweed, chopped (about ¼ cup)

1 tablespoon mushroom stock base (see Note)

MUHAMMARA

Nutty, sweet, sour, spicy, salty, and vegetal, muhammara is an out-of-this-world accompaniment. Just about anything tastes better dipped into or dolloped with this red pepper and walnut paste.

 THE PLAN: If you don't have the toasted nuts on hand, toast them first. Then pop everything into a blender or food processor in two steps, process, and serve.

In a blender (for a smoother consistency) or food processor (for a chunkier consistency), combine the peppers, walnuts, and garlic and process until well mixed. Add the oil, lemon juice, pomegranate molasses, Aleppo pepper, salt, sumac, and pepper flakes if using and process until all the ingredients are fully incorporated.

Use immediately, or transfer to an airtight container and store in the refrigerator for up to 1 week.

1 jar or can (8 oz) roasted red peppers, well drained

¾ cup walnuts, toasted (see Note, page 33)

2 cloves garlic

¼ cup extra-virgin olive oil

3 tablespoons fresh lemon juice

2 tablespoons pomegranate molasses

1 tablespoon Aleppo pepper

1 teaspoon kosher salt

1 teaspoon sumac

½ teaspoon red pepper flakes (optional)

SMOKY HUMMUS

Due in no small part to its deliciousness, you can find Middle Eastern hummus—a simple combination of chickpeas, sesame paste, lemon juice, and garlic—all over the globe. As with any super-popular food, people take all kinds of liberties with hummus these days. (We're looking at you, chocolate hummus.)

Our version sticks close to the original, but it's a little smoky (like so many things we make) and extra lemony. The consistency is on the thicker side, which allows the flavor of the beans to come through and makes it easier to spread a disproportionately large amount on a piece of toast. Depending on what we have on hand, we'll use 100 percent chickpeas, or a fifty-fifty mix with white beans, which creates a lighter, slightly creamier result.

 THE PLAN: Get everything together in a food processor and whirl until smooth.

In a food processor, combine all the ingredients and process until smooth. Taste and adjust the seasoning with a little more salt or lemon juice or a drop or two of liquid smoke if needed. Serve immediately, or store in an airtight container in the refrigerator for up to 5 days.

NOTE: Save the can liquid for making a whiskey sour (page 145) or the marshmallow fluff for the s'more brownie cupcakes (page 134).

1 cup drained canned low-sodium chickpeas

1 cup drained canned low-sodium cannellini beans

3 tablespoons extra-virgin olive oil

2 tablespoons Joyva tahini

1 tablespoon fresh lemon juice

Grated zest of 1 small lemon (about ½ teaspoon packed)

10 drops liquid smoke

½ teaspoon kosher salt

BABA GHANOUSH

We think of baba ghanoush as the Cinderella of Middle Eastern appetizers. Its (not-so-evil) stepsister, hummus, gets to go to all the parties, but baba ghanoush is secretly the most beautiful in the land. Before proceeding, know this: Chinese or Japanese eggplants make for a velvety, rich baba ghanoush every time. Italian eggplants can sometimes add some bitterness. If you can char the eggplants over an open flame, all the better. But if you need to use the broiler to make this recipe, it'll still taste amazing. Serve it with pita, chips, or raw vegetables or spread on sandwiches.

 THE PLAN: Char the eggplants, peel them, and roughly chop them. Then whisk the eggplants with the other ingredients to make this glorious dish.

Char the eggplants using one of the following three methods. The first, Blair's favorite, calls for a blow torch and tongs. Using the tongs, hold an eggplant at arm's length with your nondominant hand. Holding the torch in your other hand, turn the torch on and hold each side of the eggplant in the flame, rotating the eggplant as needed, until the eggplant is charred and blackened on all sides, 15–20 seconds on each side. Repeat with the remaining eggplants.

The second method calls for a gas stove and tongs. Turn a burner on medium-high. Using the tongs, place an eggplant directly on top of the flame. As soon as the skin on the underside is charred, carefully rotate the eggplant with the tongs to char the next side. Continue to rotate as needed until the skin is charred and blackened on all sides, 15–20 seconds on each side. Repeat with the remaining eggplants.

The third method calls for the broiler, a sheet pan, and tongs. Preheat the broiler. Arrange the eggplants on the sheet pan and place the pan on the top rack in the oven directly under the heating element. Watch the eggplants closely and rotate them with the tongs as needed until blistered and charred on each side. (You do not want to leave the eggplants in the oven any longer than needed because the interior will overcook.)

Once the eggplants are charred and blackened on all sides, transfer them to a large bowl, cover the bowl with a plate or plastic wrap, and let sit and steam for about 10 minutes. This steaming will help further loosen the skin from the flesh.

Using a paring knife, gently remove the skin from the eggplants, wiping off any stubborn black char with a wet paper towel as you go.

Roughly chop the eggplants and transfer them to a bowl. Add the oil, tahini, lemon juice and zest, and kosher salt to the eggplant and whisk together until evenly mixed. It should have a chunky consistency.

If serving immediately, transfer to a serving dish and sprinkle with the za'atar and sea salt, if using. To store, transfer to an airtight container and refrigerate for up to 1 week.

2 lb Chinese or Japanese eggplants

¼ cup extra-virgin olive oil

2 tablespoons Joyva tahini

2 tablespoons fresh lemon juice

Grated zest of 1 lemon

1½ teaspoons kosher salt

1 tablespoon za'atar (optional)

Maldon sea salt (optional)

CRUNCHY CHICKPEAS

It's almost embarrassing how much we eat these completely addictive and totally nutritious chickpeas. James, our four-year-old son, is a true believer too! They make for an amazing snack, but they also quickly turn soups and salads into a complete (and way more delicious) meal.

1 cup drained canned chickpeas

¼ cup olive oil

Kosher salt

 THE PLAN: Roast the chickpeas. Then season, cool, and serve.

Preheat the oven to 350°F. Line a sheet pan with aluminum foil.

Dry the chickpeas as much as possible with paper towels. Pile them in a mound on the center of the prepared pan. Drizzle with the oil and toss to coat evenly, then spread them in a single layer on the pan.

Roast the chickpeas, first shaking the pan and then rotating it back to front halfway through roasting, until golden brown and dry and crispy to the touch, 45–50 minutes. Remove from the oven and immediately season with the salt. Transfer to a paper towel to cool.

Enjoy immediately, or transfer to an airtight container and store at room temperature for up to 1 week.

ALABAMA WHITE SAUCE

I may live in San Francisco, but I'm an East Coast Yankee in disguise. That means I did not know what Alabama white sauce was until I met my Atlanta-born husband, and it changed my life forever (I'm talking about the sauce here, not Blair).

    The first time I had it was at Stiles Switch BBQ in Austin, Texas, when we were visiting family (yes, this was in our meat-eating years). Something clicked immediately: this was the savory sauce I always wanted but had never before experienced. What is it, you ask? Well, it's like a tangier, spicier, saucier mayonnaise that traditionally goes with Alabama barbecue.

 THE PLAN: This couldn't be easier. Just gather all the ingredients, whisk together, and serve.

In a bowl, whisk together all the ingredients until well mixed and smooth.

Use immediately, or cover tightly and refrigerate for 24 hours to allow the flavors to meld more fully. It will keep in the refrigerator for up to 2 weeks.

1 cup Just Mayo

¼ cup cider vinegar

1 tablespoon brown mustard

1 teaspoon lemon juice

1 teaspoon prepared horseradish

½ teaspoon kosher salt

½ teaspoon freshly ground black pepper

½ teaspoon garlic powder

¼ teaspoon cayenne pepper

PIZZA DOUGH

The 2020 pandemic turned Blair into a pizza-making fool. This recipe gets a ton of love around our house. The longer the dough proofs, the more character it builds, but the sweet spot is at roughly 24 hours. After about 48 hours, the yeast eats all the sugars and begins converting them to alcohol, which greatly affects the flavor of the dough.

We proof the dough overnight in the refrigerator to provide a consistent temperature, allowing the flavor to develop more gradually. We also like the addition of cornmeal, because it creates a little extra crunch in the crust.

THE PLAN: Measure everything carefully and then mix together. Proof at room temperature for 8 hours, then finish the proofing overnight in the refrigerator. Let the dough sit at room temperature for 2 hours before using.

In the bowl of a stand mixer fitted with the dough hook, sprinkle the yeast over ¼ cup of the water and let sit until foamy, about 5 minutes. Add the flour, cornmeal, salt, and the remaining ¾ cup water to the yeast mixture and mix on low speed for 1 minute. Increase the speed to medium and continue to mix until all the flour is incorporated and a soft, smooth dough forms, about 9 minutes.

Remove the bowl from the mixer stand, cover tightly with plastic wrap, and let stand in a warm place until the dough has doubled in bulk, about 8 hours. Then refrigerate the dough overnight or for at least 10 hours.

Before using, let the dough return to room temperature, about 2 hours. See the pan pizza recipe on page 102 or the flatbread recipe on page 99 for shaping and baking directions.

1 teaspoon active dry yeast

1 cup body-temperature water (95°–100°F)

2 cups "00" flour

2 tablespoons fine cornmeal

1 teaspoon kosher salt

LITTLE-FUSS PASTA DOUGH

Boxed pasta is a lot like old black-and-white movies: it has its charms, but it can be hard to enjoy fully after you've experienced the brightness and beauty of a cutting-edge color picture. Enter fresh pasta, the new-fangled television that's ruined us forever. Of course, there's a major roadblock for the plant-based diet: eggs, specifically the yolks. They're an integral part of fresh pasta, providing protein as well as fat, flavor, texture, and color. Fear not. In this recipe, we've got solutions!

Aquafaba (see sidebar) provides the protein, body, and flavor, and turmeric adds the color. Olive oil brings in the fat necessary for texture and structure. And to combine everything, Blair turns to the efficiency and consistency of a stand mixer. Next, he lets the dough rest to allow the gluten to chill out while the flour fully hydrates, then he kneads and rolls out the dough with a pasta machine rather than by hand. Studies show that allowing the dough to take a nap before using it makes a big difference in the end result. If it sleeps for less than 30 minutes, it'll be chewy, grumpy, and uneven. Pasta dough: it's just like us.

THE PLAN: Reduce the chickpea liquid. Mix the dough using a stand mixer and let rest for at least 30 minutes. Roll out the dough, cut to your desired shape and thickness, then cook and drain.

Pour the chickpea liquid into a saucepan, bring to a boil over high heat, and cook until reduced by half, about 5 minutes. Measure ¾ cup of the reduced liquid and set aside to cool for the dough. Reserve the remaining liquid for use in cocktails (page 145) or another use.

In the bowl of a stand mixer fitted with a dough hook, combine the flour, salt, and turmeric. Turn on the machine and allow the dry ingredients to mix for a few seconds, then add the ¾ cup reduced chickpea liquid and 1 tablespoon of the oil and mix on low speed until fully incorporated, about 2 minutes.

Lay a sheet of plastic wrap on a work surface and transfer the dough to the center of the sheet. Pull up the edges of the plastic wrap around the dough and apply pressure so the dough forms a ball. Wrap up the dough ball, press it into a flat disk, and let rest in the refrigerator for 30-60 minutes.

Set up your pasta machine according to the manufacturer's directions. Line a large sheet pan with parchment paper and have a kitchen towel nearby. Dust a work surface with flour. Unwrap the dough and divide it into 4 equal portions. Work with 1 portion at a time and keep the others tightly wrapped in the plastic wrap so they don't dry out. Roll out the dough on the floured surface into a long rectangle about ¼ inch thick.

Liquid from 2 cans (28 oz total) low-sodium chickpeas

2 ½ cups all-purpose or "00" flour, plus more for dusting

1 teaspoon fine sea salt

¼ teaspoon ground turmeric

1 tablespoon plus 1 teaspoon extra-virgin olive oil

Set the pasta machine rollers to the widest setting. Leading with a narrow end, feed the dough rectangle through the rollers. Now for the kneading: Fold the pasta sheet into thirds like a letter, then repeat the steps of rolling it flat with a rolling pin and feeding it through the pasta machine on the widest setting. Do this three times total.

Now, turn the knob so that the pasta roller is one setting narrower and pass the pasta through the rollers. Then turn the knob to the next narrowest setting and roll it through again. For stuffed pastas like ravioli, you will want to continue to pass the dough through narrower and narrower settings until you reach the second or third narrowest setting. For noodles, stop with the fourth narrowest setting. Lay the finished sheet of pasta on the prepared sheet pan and cover with the towel. Repeat with the remaining dough portions.

Once you have rolled out all the dough, dust the pasta sheets with flour and cut into noodles of the desired width using the pasta machine or by hand. Or leave the sheets whole and use to make stuffed pasta. Cover the pasta with the towel until ready to cook.

To cook noodles, bring a large pot of salted water to a rolling boil. Add the noodles and cook for 1–2 minutes. The timing will depend on the size of the noodles. Begin checking for doneness after 30 seconds. Watch closely, as the noodles can go from perfectly done to overcooked quickly.

Drain the noodles and toss with the remaining 1 teaspoon oil (or butter if you prefer) to prevent them from sticking together, then sauce and serve as desired.

WHAT IS AQUAFABA? You've probably noticed that the liquid that surrounds canned chickpeas is not water. It's cloudy, goopy, sometimes uneven, and—guess what—it's your new best friend. The cool thing about aquafaba is that it can perform a lot of the same tricks as eggs. Most notably, you can whip it, making it an awesome substitute for eggs in baked goods and foamy cocktails like a whiskey sour. You can even use it to make mayonnaise and pasta dough.

Index

EAT PLANTS EVERYDAY
Conceived and produced by Weldon Owen International

A WELDON OWEN PRODUCTION

PO Box 3088
San Rafael, CA 94912
www.weldonowen.com

NewSeed Press
is an imprint of Weldon Owen International

Copyright ©2021 Weldon Owen
All rights reserved, including the right of reproduction
in whole or in part in any form.

Printed in China

10 9 8 7 6 5 4 3 2 1

Library of Congress
Cataloging-in-Publication data is available.

ISBN: 978-1-68188-583-4

WELDON OWEN INTERNATIONAL

CEO Raoul Goff
Publisher Roger Shaw
Associate Publisher Amy Marr
Editorial Assistant Jourdan Plautz
Creative Director Chrissy Kwasnik
Designer Lola Villanueva
Managing Editor Lauren LePera
Production Manager Binh Au

Photographer Erin Scott
Food Stylist Lillian Kang
Prop Stylist Glenn Jenkins

Note of gratitude from the authors:
We'd like to thank Julie Hamilton for making the connection that made this book possible. Jimmy Simpson and Claire Dantine for fearlessly testing recipes for us and providing valuable feedback. Gaargi and Rishi Desai for being our cheerleaders, neighborhood family and watching James as we worked on this book. Erin Scott and her amazing crew for finally making us photogenic. And a huge shoutout to Millie Abernathy, Kate Hames, Kathryn Kuntz, Elizabeth Wells, and Katie Christopher for lending your eagle eyes and tasteful input to our layouts and copy. Finally, grazie mille to Adriano Paganinni and Alex Morgan for helping to create the vision and palate for Wildseed SF. It takes a village. This book wouldn't be in our hands without each and every one of you.

Weldon Owen wishes to thank the following people
for their generous support in producing this book:
Lesley Bruynesteyn, Elizabeth Parson, and Sharon Silva.